GOETHE'S WORLD VIEW

Goethe at 78
Painting by Josef Stieler

GOETHE'S WORLD VIEW

Presented in His Reflections and Maxims

With new English translations
and the German originals

Edited, with an introduction, by
FREDERICK UNGAR

Translated by
HEINZ NORDEN

FREDERICK UNGAR PUBLISHING CO.
New York

Second Printing

Copyright © 1963 by
Frederick Ungar Publishing Co., Inc.

Printed in the United States of America

ISBN 0-8044-6192-9
Library of Congress Catalog Card No. 63-18513

INTRODUCTION

The thoughts and sayings of Goethe here assembled represent a distillation of his wisdom and creative ideas. They embrace all spheres of life and are marked by an inner unity that stems from the dominant elements in his view of the world. The universality of Goethe's genius as a poet and thinker is equaled only by the depth and scope of his wisdom. Many people—and not by any means Germans alone—see in Goethe the most richly endowed mind ever born into our world.

"The old Eternal Genius who built the world has confided himself more to this man than to any other."—*Emerson*

"The undisputed prince of European literature."
—*Byron*

"To you more than any other I ever owe gratitude and veneration, born of the devotion of a disciple for his teacher, or rather of a son for his spiritual father."—*Carlyle*

"Posterity will marvel that there ever was such a man."—*Klinger*

"Nature has endowed him more generously than anyone since Shakespeare."—*Schiller*

"Among all German poets Goethe is the one to whom I owe most."—*Hesse*

"Of all poets and thinkers I owe most to Goethe."
—*Gide*

Testimony of this kind by the poet's contemporaries and by later critics and writers could be expanded almost at will.

A bare outline of Goethe's *Weltanschauung* * may serve to enhance the reader's fascination as well as deepen his understanding of these selections brought together from the many aspects of Goethe's work.

Not art alone but life itself constituted his mysterious mission—so Goethe put it when he was still a young man. Surely no other poet and thinker of stature so keenly felt and so fully met his responsibility to cultivate and exploit to the utmost the marvelously versatile endowments destiny had granted him. As he said on one occasion: "This craving to rear up into the air as high as possible the pyramid of my life, the base of which has been given and established for me, outweighs all else and scarcely permits of even a momentary lapse." Genius and responsibility are thus the two dominant characteristics in Goethe's character.

His autobiographical writings, his letters and recorded conversations are filled with observations on this central problem of what the Germans call *Bildung*. More than that, his *Faust,* his two *Wilhelm*

---

* There is no entirely adequate English equivalent of this term. The closest translation would probably be "world view" as used in the title of the book.

Meister novels, his *Elective Affinities* are built entirely around the question of the ethical growth of the leading characters. *Bildung* is a term that cannot be readily translated into English with a single word. To Goethe it implied the shaping of man's God-given endowments of mind and character—God being equivalent to nature—together with the sum total of his successful efforts to use them.

Yet *Bildung*, the conscious planned forming of character and spirit, must not be taken to mean that error and transgression are avoidable in the life of man. Such an assumption would ill accord with Goethe's view that all life is dominated by the law of polarity, of checks and balances between opposites. It would also conflict with his concept of the *daimon*, a word he was fond of using in a very special and fascinatingly ambivalent way. The *daimon* is on the one hand man's innermost predisposition, assigned to him by destiny at birth, and determining the quality and direction of his development. It—or he—on the other hand connotes that mysterious interweaving of destiny and character that so often unlooses man's irrational impulses, sweeping away the taboos of conventional morality, shaping life more powerfully than reason.

The *daimon* is not necessarily an impulse for evil, a baleful stroke of fate. In his later years especially, Goethe described beneficent happenings as having been fostered by his *daimon,* and he held man to be bound to guide his *daimon* in the direction of the good and the constructive. He showed in his own life that aspiration, effort and self-restraint could

7

serve to guide this obscure and mysterious force, and in his own case succeeded in shaping his life on a grander scale than any we know.

It is quite true that Goethe firmly believed man's character was essentially unalterable. He said it perhaps most clearly in his *Primeval Words* ("As on the day that to the world thee vested . . ."). Yet elsewhere he said more moderately that predisposition merely governs man's destiny "more than all else." Man is to yield to the mysterious and incomprehensible powers surrounding him only to the extent that he stands in awe of them, bearing in mind that the scope of his own free will is determined by a higher order.

The foreordained character of life is opposed by free will and moral reason. "From the power that all beings holds in fee, that man who overcomes himself casts free." Not passive acceptance of fate or of a supposed divine providence, but resolute decision and action governed by reason are the way to a practical solution of the problems life poses. "The fabric of this world is formed of necessity and chance; man's reason stands between the two and takes their measure."

Here too, then, we see the principle of polarity that governed Goethe's approach to the world, the law of checks and balances prevailing throughout life and nature. We shall come back again to this basic notion, to which Goethe reduces all happenings in life, in which he sees "life's everlasting formula" and the "true pulse of life."

It is impossible to grasp Goethe's thinking fully

unless we take into account his relationship to nature, which lies at the heart of his philosophy. His contemplation of nature is based on precise observation of phenomena. He sought to grasp the forces that set them in motion, never let his thinking wander from things and become speculative. "Do not look beyond the phenomena; they are the doctrine." Or, as he put it in poetic enhancement: "A colorful reflection only, yet 'tis life itself."

His research, his immersion in nature did not pursue the aim of merely explaining individual natural phenomena. His real goal was to perceive, in the flow of ever shifting single events, the underlying law and thus the imprint of God.

In Goethe's view man is not the center of the universe but only a product of the general creative power, albeit the highest. For Goethe God and nature were one, and he could conceive of nothing that did not have its origin in the same divine source. His life-long scientific quest—he devoted more time to his scientific experiments and publications than to all of his poetic and prose works—was meant to unveil the secrets of nature to him. It was much more than a pastime—it was a vocation, a vital necessity. Only insight into nature could afford him that world picture that alone satisfied his mind and spirit. "That I discern how in its core,/The world is joined forevermore," he writes in *Faust*.

His immersion in nature was not primarily directed toward fathoming things as such, but rather the evolutionary laws and the forces that made them what they are, for these forces that move the physical

world he conceived to be identical with those that are at work in the mind and in the ethical behavior of man. What Goethe strove after was insight into the cosmic laws that govern man as they do all manifestations of nature. This was to give him a deeper understanding of man's place in the universe, his potentialities and goals.

Goethe viewed nature as a seamless entity, obeying dynamic principles that could be reduced to law. Against this unchanging background, however, phenomena themselves shift and vary in everlasting cycles. Units are subdivided, only to merge back into one. In these ceaseless processes of division and union Goethe saw the archetypal phenomenon of polarity that governs all creatures. The mutual interaction of opposed forces, attraction and repulsion, is the essential principle underlying all that stirs and happens in nature. It is the source of all life.

This polar rhythm of life is symbolically signified with particular clarity in the contraction (systole) and expansion (diastole) of the heart and the equally rhythmic function of breathing, inhaling and exhaling being mutually interdependent. One function would cease without the other, and with it life itself. Thus, seemingly negative counteractions are anything but harmful—they are an imperative of nature.

Goethe starts out with observation of the single organism and works up to the general, to the type. He poses a question of the origin of single orga-

10

nisms and their development from primeval forms. He contemplates the stem of a plant, and his formative glance sees, in shapes as diversified as root, leaf, blossom and fruit, only the variation of a unified essential form, the leaf. His eye rests on the spinal column of higher vertebrates and perceives a similar metamorphosis, shaping the ideal vertebra into pelvis, vertebrae, jaws and skull. He observes light and darkness through a turbid medium, and they split up into colors. Goethe sees all of nature filled with such archephenomena dispersed into colorful multiplicity.

We must keep in mind, however, that the diversification of the unified idea into a multiplicity of phenomena and, conversely, the synthesis of related phenomena into one idea, are processes within pure intuition and not causal processes in themselves. Goethe did not realize this until it was brought home to him by Schiller in that fateful discussion that started their friendship.

In other respects, too, Goethe found a complementary antagonism in all occurrences. "To separate, to unite, to indulge in the general, to persist in the special," this is the heartbeat of life everywhere in the universe. "Rising and passing, creation and annihilation, birth and death, joy and grief, they all work meshed in one another." He called polarity "the eternal formula of life." The point in question here, however, is not an antagonism of a hostile, exclusive kind, as in a logical antithesis where only one of two contradictory statements can be correct,

but a creative opposition, which tries to effect an equilibrium out of itself "With gentle weight and counterweight nature balances to and fro."

The doctrine of creative opposites as a basic law of nature, as the cause that gave rise to matter and perpetuates it, is as old as philosophy itself. Among the Greek philosophers it was represented preeminently by Heraclitus and Aristotle. In the philosophic thought of Goethe's time the principle of polarity was in great vogue. It was influential in shaping the natural philosophy of Schelling, which drew heavily on Kant. Goethe described this principle as one of his earliest convictions.

In addition to the everlasting sequence of ebb and flow, of growth and decline, Goethe recognized a second archprinciple of nature. This is the conception of norms, or ideals, which ensure that sameness is not indefinitely perpetuated but rather that the course of nature is marked by a gradually rising line of development, which he often called enhancement (*Steigerung*).

Both of these principles apply throughout creation and thus include man. The counterpoise of evil is necessary, if good is to come into effect. The capacity of sane men to strive upward, to perfect themselves morally, mankind's progressive tendency toward humanity—these demonstrate the principle of enhancement. Goethe was fully aware of the power of these two fundamental principles in his own growth.

Toward philosophy in the narrower sense Goethe displayed considerable aloofness, if not aversion. In-

terested as he was in all areas of knowledge, he also delved into the philosophic sytems of his time—which indeed saw the flowering of German philosophy. It was he who, as prime minister of the Duchy of Saxe-Weimar, appointed the leading thinkers of his time to chairs at the University of Jena—Fichte, Schelling, Hegel—yet nothing was further from his mind than to evolve a philosophical system of his own. He found epistemology confusing and unprofitable. Abstract thought was not his way of grasping the essential nature of the world. The affective powers must also come into full play, and even they are inadequate to discern the infinite, which lies beyond human comprehension und must remain inaccessible.

Yet truth, Goethe held, was more closely approached through the emotions and the senses than through abstract thought. Thought must not supplant apperception, though it may contribute toward enhancing instinct and emotion, putting them on a better foundation. To break through into real comprehension of the world, apperception and thought must blend into one. Only the fusion of sensual and spiritual forces is equal to encompassing the world of phenomena, which itself represents a merging of spirit and matter, for the laws that govern the universe also govern human cognition.

Although Goethe agrees with other philosophers on certain details—in particular with Spinoza's pantheism—his intellectual approach of viewing individual problems in the total context of his *Weltanschauung*, of seeing the finite within the infinite,

differs radically from all the philosophical systems of his age.

He never looked for God beyond nature, professing instead the unity of God and nature; and he felt in consequence that all systems of speculative philosophy did violence to nature. Similarly, any philosophic justification of morality was foreign to his nature, for he viewed ethical thought in man as a manifestation of nature, in which God was revealed as in all natural phenomena.

The question whether the world has any meaning had little meaning itself to Goethe, who was convinced that nothing living in the world is a means to an end, but that it is an end in itself. The world thus has meaning when each individual creature fulfills its purpose, and man too must rest content with this state of things. The purpose of man's life is to develop the good within him and to resist the evil that opposes the good—in Goethe's view human nature, in addition to being tainted with outright evil, or what religion calls original sin, must "also be credited with original virtue." Man's peculiar disposition is to strive for ethical perfection, and only in the pursuit of this aspiration can he attain harmony with the infinite.

Goethe rejected the traditional forms of religion, though he did seek genuine religious experience, which, he felt, was not at odds with his scientific approach. A sense of the majesty of the universe, recognition of man's narrow limitations, submission to the will of an incomprehensible power that "must be quietly venerated"—these attitudes seemed to

Goethe appropriate and conducive to man's position within the infinite cosmos. He wished to see religion freed of its dogmatic shackles, guided into higher and purer forms that would satisfy both emotion and reason.

Goethe's creed was a creed of nature. His ethics were humanity idealized. Since man is the highest manifestation of the divine on earth, the ideal to be striven for is the highest embodiment of all that is human.

Goethe dealt with man's yearning for the good life among his fellowmen in his last great novel, *Wilhelm Meister,* more specifically in the chapter entitled "The Pedagogic Province." His purpose here was to represent idealized humanity as the only possible basis of society. What he called for was the useful and productive life, built around respect for the vital interests of one's fellows.

The crucial element to him was the communal spirit, without which man's social life, no matter how well organized, was doomed to frustration and failure. There was no room for economic theory in Goethe's social thinking, since he was convinced that mere outward changes in social relationships could not bring about enduring and desirable changes in human relationships. Economic changes would merely distract attention from the central problem, which was ethical in nature. This was nothing less than the struggle to make the basic values of occidental humanism prevail throughout the world. Humanism alone bade fair to give rise to that enduring harmony in human social bonds

that might reconcile conflicts among individuals, classes and creeds. The ideal society could be achieved only through the ethical aspirations of the individual.

To learn "renunciation"—that is seen as the moral basis for a useful life. This concept is of major importance for Goethe—*Wilhelm Meister's Wanderings* is subtitled *The Renouncers*. Renunciation did not mean to him passive submission to fate, as might be thought, but rather serene acceptance of the fact that life has its disappointments as well as its fulfillments, that man must learn to indulge or curb his desires, as the case may be and as reason and responsibility dictate.

The position of the student in "The Pedagogic Province" is determined by the ethical quality of his behavior. He must maintain, or be converted to, high ethical standards if he is to attain his academic goal. What is esteemed most highly is to establish a relationship of harmony with one's fellows. Only he who has learned to respect others in a spirit of friendship can come to respect himself and thus attain inner freedom. "Reverence for self" is rooted in a vision of the evolutionary potential of the self. It is the means for realizing the obligation imposed on man, to develop his potential to the fullest.

What is essential is that the student accept limitations to his activity, in order to strengthen himself for the tasks of life, and to make himself more useful to society. All men should first learn a craft, acquire a practical skill. He who strives without a set goal accomplishes nothing. Only voluntary lim-

itation paves the way for great achievement. Dilettantism is not only ethically dubious but incompatible with true culture, while practical specialization represents a moral principle of education. "To know and practice a craft lends greater culture than half-knowledge a hundred times over."

Yet work directed toward practical utility is by no means to be separated from reason and reflection. Action and thought, work and contemplation are to remain perpetually interrelated. This is the sum of all practical wisdom.

Goethe's endeavors are here aimed at an educational system unlike that of Plato, directed by the state and seeking to create an elite of talent. Under his dispensation bourgeois society entrusts practical humanists with the task of education, and they are in turn to train the young as practical humanists. Morality based on fellowship is to be at the heart of this system, but side by side with it the emphasis is on learning a skill that will benefit society. Goethe's efforts must be viewed as an outgrowth of his concern with the problem of creating a sound social order, in keeping with the needs and requirements of the new age that loomed ahead.

Goethe transplanted "The Pedagogic Province," his utopia of an ideal society, into his own time. Perhaps he meant to imply that it could be realized in any age, just so long as man had attained the ethical maturity required for its realization. He was under no illusions, however, about its early achievement; he was fully aware that in actual fact such a society could be realized only in the far distant future. "The

Pedagogic Province" is his legacy to that time, and as such its significance will endure.

Goethe lived to see the first stirrings of socialism, but he held aloof from the political slogans of the day. He was convinced that salvation could be expected only from the individual and his quest for moral and spiritual perfection. Privacy, the basic rights of the individual, must be protected against the swelling power of the mass will. To have all action guided by the welfare of the masses seemed to him futile and against the interests of society, which could be advanced only through the integrity and achievements of the individual.

In this respect, as in his views on violent upheaval generally, Goethe must be classed with the conservative thinkers opposed to the revolutionary approach. Yet he was scarcely conservative in his views on the goals of the social order, which he wished to see serving the needs of all, ruled by the principles of mutual aid and individual service to the community. Thus Goethe's conservatism is infused with a social humanism concerned not with one class or one nation but with the self-realization of all mankind.

Faust and *Wilhelm Meister* have often been regarded as complements, one to the other. *Faust* embodies the arrogant denial of all human limitations, while *Wilhelm Meister* accepts their necessity, indeed posits that self-discipline, that channeling of passion, in short, that essential attitude toward life which Goethe called renunciation.

Throughout almost his entire life Goethe continued to be preoccupied with these two works, which he

concluded only shortly before his death. Significantly enough, it is Albert Schweitzer who points out that Faust, demanding ultimate knowledge from the world spirit, ends up wresting land from the sea to feed people; while Wilhelm Meister sees his destiny in serving as physician to a group of emigrants seeking to establish a new society in the faraway New World.

It is well to remember in this connection that for almost a full decade Goethe all but had to forego his creative work in order to devote himself to the practical tasks that fell to him as prime minister of the Duchy of Saxe-Weimar. He had to salvage a disorganized state exchequer, build roads and bridges, reopen abandoned mines, run the school system and do much else. Later on also he devoted a substantial part of his time to official duties.

This juxtaposition of duties imposed by the "demands of the day" and of free creative work may well serve as an exhortation never to ignore the creative challenge because of the often dreary workaday tasks exacted by the struggle for existence. Here again it is the unity of theory and practice, the inward sincerity of character, that are so impressive in Goethe. They command the reader's confidence, as they did that of his contemporaries. Let us listen here to but one of the many witnesses who enjoyed a personal relationship with him and testified to the greatness of his character. On November 23, 1800, Schiller wrote the Countess Schimmelmann:

"I have now known Goethe for six years and I regard my acquaintance with him as having con-

ferred more benefit upon me than anything else in my life. I scarcely need tell you anything about the man's mind, and you recognize his stature as a poet. . . . In my firm conviction no other poet even remotely approaches him in depth and delicacy of feeling, in naturalness, truth and sheer creative power. Nature has endowed him more generously than anyone since Shakespeare. Beyond these natural endowments, moreover, he has enhanced his stature through ceaseless study and research more than anyone else. For twenty long years he has shunned no effort to delve into the three realms of nature, and he has plumbed the very depths of science. He accumulated major findings in physics, anticipating in his solitary way discoveries about which much ado is made nowadays. . . . What other poet comes even close to him in such profundity of knowledge?—yet he has devoted a large part of his life to his ministerial duties, which are neither petty nor insignificant just because the Duchy is small.

"Yet it is not these outstanding intellectual achievements that bind me to him. I would be content to worship his genius from afar—but for the fact that he happens to be, of all the men I have ever personally known, the one whom I treasure above all others. I may confidently say that in the six years I have spent with him I have never had reason to doubt his integrity for a moment. There is a lofty truthfulness and simplicity in his nature, and the most serious concern for what is good and right. Perhaps that is why gossips, hypocrites and hairsplitters always feel ill at ease in his presence."

Sincerity was the essence of Goethe's character. He never evaded a duty or responsibility that came his way. He felt a deep need to serve. His exhortations to others were meant no less for himself and made him one of mankind's great teachers, however little he may have meant to be didactic. Seldom has a writer so simply and understandably formulated thoughts of such depth and import. Few poets and thinkers can be read with greater profit to one's understanding of the world.

Goethe is rightly accounted the greatest German poet, the last poet of topmost rank since Shakespeare and the last great universal genius whom the West produced; yet in assessing his influence it must be borne in mind that the effects of pure lyricism—in which he scaled the heights—are limited, while his prose works reach only a relatively small number of sophisticated readers, as indeed Goethe had foreseen.

What really puts us under Goethe's spell is the story of his life, his profound humanity. This has been eloquently pictured a thousand times and become the intellectual property of a broad public. Goethe carried within himself strong temptations to burst through his self-imposed limitations. Upheavals in his personal life repeatedly threatened to destroy him. Yet he never lost his capacity for "showing himself upright" and thus keeping the image of man intact within himself. His outbursts of despair, loneliness and renunciation give us a moving picture of the toil and effort, the sorrow and suffering that were not lacking in his life, and this makes him appear all

the more human. His life thus becomes a symbol of all human existence, and to immerse oneself in it serves to aid self-understanding and mobilize latent reserves of power.

His all-embracing humanitarianism is especially marked in *Wilhelm Meister's Wanderings* and the utterances of his old age, though his outlook was cosmopolitan all his life and he always opposed super-patriotism. "We must make a part of our life the concept of a devotion owed to all mankind (*Welt-frömmigkeit*), we must give practical application on the broadest scale to our deep-felt humane senti-ments, we must sweep along all of mankind, not merely those closest to us." Goethe was convinced that everything of significance in art and science be-longed to all mankind; and it was his anxious concern and confident hope at the same time that mankind join hands in a spirit of tolerance and brotherhood.

He saw the emergence of a new world. That he was deeply interested in *the* New World, in the young country of America, is seen from thoughts and utterances included here. Not a few leading Amer-icans of his time visited him in Weimar, a politically insignificant spot which he made the cultural center of Europe. They were all impressed with his lively interest in America and the scope of his information about it. He not only at one time busied himself with plans for writing a history of America—in his time a less ambitious undertaking than today—but he said more than once that he might not have resisted the temptation of starting a new life in America, had he been twenty years younger.

In Goethe's thinking great literature, as the highest expression of the creative spirit of a nation was destined to serve the union of all nations, in the spirit of world-wide humanity. This cosmopolitan ideal, the favorite notion of Goethe's last years, was to be realized in his concept of a true world literature. To him this meant a literature that in content and creative value would rise above the spheres of national life, a sublime heritage belonging not to the nation producing it but to all mankind.

As we know, this hope of Goethe's was not fulfilled. The modern world has failed to realize his image of man, not because it is or ever could become obsolete, but because man's humanization, in which alone Goethe saw salvation, has made such slow progress, lapsing again and again into inhumanity.

Dare we hope that Goethe's work, from which not merely the individual but all nations might cull much practical wisdom as well as idealism, will some day achieve that world-wide influence for which it is destined? The very question leads us back to Goethe, whose deep faith in the inexhaustibly regenerative powers of nature, and thus of the creative spirit of man, summons us once again:

"We bid you, have hope!"

F.U.

Das schönste Glück des denkenden Menschen ist, das Erforschliche erforscht zu haben und das Un-erforschliche ruhig zu verehren.

The highest happiness of man as a thinking being is to have probed what is knowable and quietly to revere what is unknowable.

Wir können bei Betrachtung des Weltgebäudes in seiner weitesten Ausdehnung, in seiner letzten Teilbarkeit uns der Vorstellung nicht erwehren, daß dem Ganzen eine Idee zum Grunde liege, wonach Gott in der Natur, die Natur in Gott, von Ewigkeit zu Ewigkeit, schaffen und wirken möge.

Glaube ist Liebe zum Unsichtbaren, Vertrauen aufs Unmögliche, Unwahrscheinliche.

Es gibt keine schönere Gottesverehrung als die, zu der man kein Bild bedarf, die bloß aus dem Wechselgespräch mit der Natur in unserem Busen entspringt.

Natur! Wir sind von ihr umgeben und umschlungen —unvermögend, aus ihr herauszutreten, und unvermögend, tiefer in sie hineinzukommen. Ungebeten und ungewarnt nimmt sie uns in den Kreislauf ihres Tanzes auf und treibt sich mit uns fort, bis wir ermüdet sind und ihrem Arme entfallen.

Die Natur ist doch das einzige Buch, das auf allen Blättern großen Gehalt bietet.

Als wenn die Außenwelt dem, der Augen hat, nicht überall die geheimsten Gesetze täglich und nächtlich offenbarte! In dieser Konsequenz des unendlich Mannigfaltigen sehe ich Gottes Handschrift am allerdeutlichsten.

In contemplating the world edifice in its farthest expanse, its ultimate divisibility, we can scarcely avoid the thought that the whole of it is founded on an idea by which God creates and works in nature, nature in God, from everlasting to everlasting.

Faith is love of the invisible, trust in the impossible, in the improbable.

There is no finer divine worship than that which requires no image, which springs solely from the dialogue with nature in our breast.

Nature! We are enveloped and embraced by her, incapable of emerging from her and incapable of entering her more deeply. Unbidden and unwarned, she receives us into the circuits of her dance, drifting onward with us herself, until we grow tired and drop from her arms.

Nature, after all, is the only book, every page of which offers a content of greatness.

As though the world outside did not, to him who has eyes, every day and every night reveal its innermost laws! In this consistency of infinite variety I see God's handwriting most plainly.

Vom unzugänglichen Gebirge über die Einöde, die kein Fuß betrat, bis ans Ende des unbekannten Ozeans, weht der Geist des Ewigschaffenden, und freut sich jeden Staubs, der ihn vernimmt und lebt.

Ich bin geneigter als jemand, noch eine Welt außer der sichtbaren zu glauben.

Beseelte Gott den Vogel nicht mit diesem allmächtigen Trieb gegen seine Jungen, und ginge das gleiche nicht durch alles Lebendige der ganzen Natur, die Welt würde nicht bestehen können. So aber ist die göttliche Kraft überall verbreitet, und die ewige Liebe überall wirksam.

Der liebe Gott könnte uns recht in Verlegenheit setzen, wenn er uns die Geheimnisse der Natur sämtlich offenbarte, wir wüßen für Unteilnahme und Langerweile nicht, was wir anfangen sollten.

Geheimnisvoll am lichten Tag
Läßt sich Natur des Schleiers nicht berauben,
Und was sie deinem Geist nicht offenbaren mag,
Das zwingst du ihr nicht ab mit Hebeln und mit
    Schrauben.

Müsset im Naturbetrachten
Immer eins wie alles achten.
Nichts ist drinnen, nichts ist draußen:
Denn was innen, das ist außen.
So ergreift ohne Säumnis
Heilig öffentlich Geheimnis.

From inaccessible mountain range by way of desert untrod by human foot to the ends of the unknown seas, the breath of the everlasting creative spirit is felt, rejoicing over every speck of dust that hearkens to it and lives.

I am more inclined than some to believe in a world beyond the visible.

Did not God inspire the bird with this all-powerful drive to care for its young, and did not the same spirit pervade all living things in nature, the world could not endure. Thus indeed is the divine power scattered everywhere, and love everlasting in action far and near.

God could indeed cause us embarrassment if he revealed all of nature's mysteries to us. We would scarcely know what to do for boredom and indifference.

Mysterious in light of day,
Her veils doth Nature freely loosen never,
And all the secrets she will not to thee display
Thou shalt not worm away from her with prize and
    lever.

In your nature observation
One and all want equal station.
Nothing's inside, nothing's outside.
For the inside is the outside.
Grasp without procrastination
Patent-occult revelation.

Was hieße wohl die Natur ergründen?
Gott ebenso außen wie innen zu finden.

Was wär' ein Gott, der nur von außen stieße,
Im Kreis das All am Finger laufen ließe?
Ihm ziemt's, die Welt im Innern zu bewegen,
Natur in Sich, Sich in Natur zu hegen,
So daß, was in Ihm lebt und webt und ist,
Nie Seine Kraft, nie Seinen Geist vermißt.

Wär' nicht das Auge sonnenhaft,
Die Sonne könnt' es nie erblicken.
Läg' nicht in uns des Gottes eigne Kraft,
Wie könnt' uns Göttliches entzücken?

Am farbigen Abglanz haben wir das Leben.

Man such nur nichts hinter den Phänomenen, sie
selbst sind die Lehre.

Alles Vergängliche ist nur ein Gleichnis.

Und so lang du das nicht hast,
Dieses: Stirb und Werde!
Bist du nur ein trüber Gast
Auf der dunklen Erde.

What is it we probers of Nature are seeking?
Out there the God whom within we hear speaking!

What would a God be who but gave the world
A push to have it spin around His finger?
Him it behooves to move things from within
Comprising Nature and comprised by Her,
So that what in Him grows and flows and is
Must share the strength and spirit that are His.

Were not the eye born of the sun,
It could not shine in sunlike splendor.
Had our life not in God's life begun,
How could to things divine we seek surrender?

A colorful reflection only, yet 'tis life itself.

Do not look beyond the phenomena; they are the
doctrine.

Everything temporal is but a parable.

And till you have stood this test:
"Die, and come to birth!"
You remain a sorry guest
On this gloomy earth.

Ich kann überhaupt nicht begreifen, wie man hat glauben können, daß Gott durch Bücher und Geschichten zu uns spreche. Wem die Welt nicht unmittelbar eröffnet, was sie für ein Verhältnis zu ihm hat, wem sein Herz nicht sagt, was er sich und andern schuldig ist, der wird es wohl schwerlich aus Büchern erfahren, die eigentlich nur geschickt sind, unsern Irrtümern Namen zu geben.

It is quite beyond me how anyone can believe God speaks to us in books and stories. If the world does not directly reveal to us our relationship to it, if our hearts fail to tell us what we owe ourselves and others, we shall assuredly not learn it from books, which are at best designed but to give names to our errors.

Nicht das macht frei, daß wir nichts über uns anerkennen wollen, sondern eben, daß wir etwas verehren, das über uns ist. Denn indem wir es verehren, heben wir uns zu ihm hinauf und legen an den Tag, daß wir selber das Höhere in uns tragen und wert sind, seinesgleichen zu sein.

Ich kann von Gott nichts weiter wissen, als wozu mich der beschränkte Gesichtskreis von sinnlichen Wahrnehmungen auf dieser Erde berechtigt, und das ist wenig genung. Dadurch ist aber dem Glauben keine Schranke gesetzt. Im Gegenteil kann bei der Unmittelbarkeit göttlicher Gefühle in uns der Fall eintreten, daß das Wissen als Stückwerk erscheint, daß jede Betrachtung unvolkommen bleibt und eben darum erst durch den Glauben ihre volle Ergänzung erhält. Man muß nur von dem Grundsatz ausgehen: daß Wissen und Glauben nicht dazu da sind, einander aufzuheben, sondern einander zu ergänzen, dann wird schon überall das Richtige ausgemittelt werden.

Wir müssen einsehen lernen, daß wir dasjenige, was wir im Einfachsten geschaut und erkannt, im Zusammengesetzten supponieren und glauben müssen. Denn das Einfache verbirgt sich im Mannigfaltigen, und da ist's, wo bei mir der Glaube eintritt, der nicht der Anfang, sondern das Ende allen Wissens ist.

Echt oder unecht sind bei Dingen der Bibel gar wunderliche Fragen. Was ist echt als das ganz

We are not made free by refusing to acknowledge anything above us, but by venerating something that is above us; for by worshiping it, we exalt ourselves to its level and give proof that the sublime dwells within us and that we are worthy to be its peer.

I can know nothing further of God but what the limited compass of sensory perception on this earth allows me, which is precious little. But that sets no limit to faith. On the contrary, in the face of the immediacy of divine sentiments within us knowledge may happen to appear piecemeal, every bit of cognition to remain incomplete and for that very reason to achieve fullness only by faith. One need but proceed from the principle that knowledge and faith exist not to cancel but to complement each other, and all will fall into its proper place.

We must learn to accept that what we have seen and perceived in the simplest context we must come to presume and believe to apply to the most complex; for the simple is hidden within the complex, and that is where in my case faith commences, which is the end of all knowledge rather than its beginning.

The concept of genuine or spurious when applied to matters of the Bible raises very curious questions.

Vortreffliche, das mit der reinsten Natur und Vernunft in Harmonie steht und noch heute unserer höchsten Entwicklung dient! Und was ist unecht als das Absurde, Hohle, Dumme, was keine Frucht bringt, wenigstens keine gute! . . . Ich halte die Evangelien alle vier für durchaus echt, denn es ist in ihnen der Abglanz einer Hoheit wirksam, die von der Person Christi ausging und die so göttlicher Art, wie nur je auf Erden das Göttliche erschienen ist. Fragt man mich, ob es in meiner Natur sei, ihm anbetende Ehrfurcht zu erweisen, so sage ich: durchaus! Ich beuge mich vor ihm, als der göttlichen Offenbarung des höchsten Prinzips der Sittlichkeit. Fragt man mich, ob es in meiner Natur sei, die Sonne zu verehren, so sage ich abermals: durchaus! Denn sie ist gleichfalls eine Offenbarung des Höchsten, und zwar die mächtigste, die uns Erdenkindern wahrzunehmen vergönnt ist. Ich anbete in ihr das Licht und die zeugende Kraft Gottes, wodurch allein wir leben, weben und sind, und alle Pflanzen und Tiere mit uns. Fragt man mich aber, ob ich geneigt sei, mich vor einem Daumenknochen des Apostels Petri oder Pauli zu bücken, so sage ich: Verschont mich und bleibt mir mit euren Absurditäten vom Leibe!

Wenn man die Leute reden hört, so sollte man fast glauben, sie seien der Meinung, Gott habe sich seit jener alten Zeit ganz in die Stille zurückgezogen und der Mensch wäre jetzt ganz auf eigene Füsse gestellt und müsse sehen, wie er ohne Gott und sein tägliches unsichtbares Anhauchen zurechtkomme. In religiö-

What is genuine but the thoroughly splendid, which stands in harmony with purest nature and reason and still today serves our highest development! And what is spurious but the absurd, hollow and stupid, which bears no fruit—at least no good fruit! . . . Yet I regard all four Gospels as quite genuine, for in them is evident the reflected splendor of the sublime power which emanated from the person of Christ, and His nature which was as divine as ever the divine has appeared on earth. If I am asked whether it be my nature to render Him prayerful reverence, my answer is: Absolutely! I bow before Him as a divine manifestation of the highest principle of morality. If I am asked whether it be in my nature to venerate the sun, I answer again: Absolutely! For it too is a manifestation of the highest, and is indeed the most powerful one granted us children of the earth to perceive. In it I worship the light, and the procreative power of God, through which solely we live, and move and have our being, and all the plants and animals along with us. But if I am asked whether I am inclined to prostrate myself before a thumb bone of the Apostle Peter or Paul, then I say, Spare me and stay away with your absurdities!

To hear people talk, one might almost believe they think God has altogether withdrawn into seclusion since those ancient times, while man is now entirely on his own and must see how he manages without God and his daily invisible inspiration. In matters

37

sen und moralischen Dingen gibt man noch allenfalls eine göttliche Einwirkung zu, allein in Dingen der Wissenschaft und Künste glaubt man, es sei lauter Irdisches und nichts weiter als ein Produkt rein menschlicher Kräfte.

Gott hat sich nach den bekannten imaginierten sechs Schöpfungstagen keineswegs zur Ruhe begeben, vielmehr ist er noch fortwährend wirksam wie am ersten. Diese plumpe Welt aus einfachen Elementen zusammenzusetzen und sie jahraus, jahrein in den Strahlen der Sonne rollen zu lassen, hätte ihm sicher wenig Spaß gemacht, wenn er nicht den Plan gehabt hätte, sich auf dieser materiellen Unterlage eine Pflanzschule für eine Welt von Geistern zu gründen. So ist er nun fortwährend in höheren Naturen wirksam, um die geringeren heranzuziehen.

Man streitet viel und wird viel streiten über Nutzen und Schaden der Bibelverbreitung. Mir ist klar: schaden wird sie wie bisher, dogmatisch und phantastisch gebraucht; nutzen wie bisher, didaktisch und gefühlvoll aufgenommen.

Deshalb ist die Bibel ein ewig wirksames Buch, weil, solange die Welt steht, niemand auftreten und sagen wird: ich begreife es im Ganzen und verstehe es im Einzelnen. Wir aber sagen bescheiden: im Ganzen ist es ehrwürdig und im Einzelnen anwendbar.

of religion and morals one still grudgingly admits God plays a role, but in matters of science and art all is held to be secular, nothing more than the product of purely human forces.

God has by no means gone into retirement after the six well-known imaginary days of creation but rather continues as busy as on the first. To put together this coarse world from simple elements and allow it to roll on year after year in the rays of the sun would have surely given him less pleasure, had he not had a plan to found a nursery for a world of the spirit on this material foundation. Thus he carries on his work in higher natures, to draw aloft the lesser ones.

There is and always will be much controversy over the good or harm done by widespread Bible-reading. It seems clear to me that, taken dogmatically and fancifully, it does much harm, as it has done hitherto; while taken didactically and sentimentally it is as useful as it has always been.

Hence the Bible is an ever effective book; for as long as the world stands none dare say: I comprehend it in whole and understand it in part. Let us modestly assert that it is awe-inspiring in the whole and applicable in part.

Du findest nichts schöner als das Evangelium. Ich finde tausend geschriebene Blätter alter und neuer von Gott begnadeter Menschen ebenso schön, und der Menschheit nützlich und unentbehrlich.

Ich ehre die Religion, ich fühle, daß sie manchem Ermatteten Stab, manchem Verschmachtenden Erquickung ist. Nur—kann sie denn, muß sie denn das einem jeden sein? Wenn du die große Welt ansiehst, so siehst du Tausende, denen sie es nicht war, Tausende, denen sie es nicht sein wird, gepredigt oder ungepredigt.

Des religiösen Gefühls wird sich kein Mensch erwehren, dabei aber ist es ihm unmöglich, solches in sich allein zu verarbeiten, deswegen sucht er oder macht sich Proselyten. Das letztere ist meine Art nicht, das erstere aber hab' ich treulich durchgeführt, und von Erschaffung der Welt an keine Konfession gefunden, zu der ich mich völlig hätte bekennen mögen.

Und warum sollte ich hier nicht gestehen, daß mir bei jener großen Forderung: *man solle seine Feinde lieben*, das Wort *lieben* gemißbraucht oder wenigstens in sehr uneigentlichem Sinne gebraucht scheine, wogegen ich mit viel Überzeugung gerne jenen weisen Spruch wiederhole: daß man einen guten Haushälter hauptsächlich daran erkenne, wenn er sich sich des Widerwärtigen vorteilhaft zu bedienen wisse.

You find nothing more beautiful than the Gospel, while I find a thousand pages written by men inspired by God throughout the ages equally beautiful, and useful and indispensable to mankind.

I honor religion—I sense that it is as a staff to many who are weary, balm to many who languish. The point is: need it, must it perform these services for all? Look at the world at large and you will see thousands whom it never so served and thousands whom it never will, whether they have been preached to or not.

No one can altogether deny religious sentiment, nor can he cope with it alone, hence he seeks out or makes converts. To make such is not my nature, but I have painstakingly sought them out, yet found no creed from world's beginning to which I might have given full allegiance.

And why should I not here confess that the word *love* in that great challenge, *Love thy enemies,* seems to me to be misused, or at least to be used in a meaning very different from the usual? I am, on the other hand, quite fond of repeating, with much conviction, the wise saying that a good husbandman is recognized chiefly from his ability to turn even the untoward to his advantage.

Was mich nämlich von der Brüdergemeinde sowie von andern werten Christenseelen absonderte, war dasselbige, worüber die Kirche schon mehr als einmal in Spaltung geraten war. Ein Teil behauptete, daß die menschliche Natur durch den Sündenfall dergestalt verdorben sei, daß auch bis in ihren innersten Kern nicht das mindeste Gute an ihr zu finden, deshalb der Mensch auf seine eignen Kräfte durchaus Verzicht zu tun und alles von der Gnade und ihrer Einwirkung zu erwarten habe. Der andere Teil gab zwar die erblichen Mängel der Menschen sehr gern zu, wollte aber der Natur inwendig noch einen gewissen Keim zugestehn, welcher, durch göttliche Gnade belebt, zu einem frohen Baume geistiger Glückseligkeit emporwachsen könne. Von dieser letztern Überzeugung war ich aufs innigste durchdrungen, ohne es selbst zu wissen, obwohl ich mich mit Mund und Feder zu dem Gegenteile bekannt hatte.

Wir wissen gar nicht, was wir Luthern und der Reformation im allgemeinen alles zu danken haben. Wir sind frei geworden von den Fesseln geistiger Borniertheit, wir sind infolge unserer fortwachsenden Kultur fähig geworden, zur Quelle zurückzukehren und das Christentum in seiner Reinheit zu fassen. Wir haben wieder den Mut, mit festen Füßen auf Gottes Erde zu stehen und uns in unserer gottbegabten Menschennatur zu fühlen. Mag die geistige Kultur nur immer fortschreiten, mögen die Naturwissenschaften in immer breiterer Ausdehnung und

For what sundered me from the congregation as well as from other worthy Christian souls was the very thing on which the Church has split more than once. Part of it maintained that by the Fall of Man human nature became so depraved that not the least good is to be found in it to its innermost core, wherefore man must utterly renounce his own powers, putting all his hope in the workings of grace. The other part, while quite readily admitting the deficiencies in man's heritage, still conceded to inmost nature a certain germ which, inspired by divine grace, could grow up into a joyful tree of spiritual bliss. Without myself knowing it, I was intimately pervaded by this latter conviction, though with word and pen I had professed the contrary.

We really do not know all the things for which we owe thanks to Luther and the Reformation in general. We have been freed of the shackles of narrow-mindedness. As a result of our continually growing culture we have become capable of returning to the source and comprehending Christianity in its purity. Once again we have the courage to stand firmly on God's earth and to be aware of our God-given human nature. May cultural pursuits hereafter ever continue to advance; may the sciences encompass ever-widening circles and profounder

Tiefe wachsen und der menschliche Geist sich erweitern, wie er will,—über die Hoheit und sittliche Kultur des Christentums, wie es in den Evangelien schimmert und leuchtet, wird es nicht hinauskommen!

Je tüchtiger aber wir Protestanten in edler Entwickelung voranschreiten, desto schneller werden die Katholiken folgen. Sobald sie sich von der immer Zeit ergriffen fühlen, *müssen* sie nach, sie mögen sich stellen, wie sie wollen, und es wird dahin kommen, daß endlich alles nur eins ist.

Auch das leidige protestantische Sektenwesen wird weiter um sich greifenden großen Aufklärung der aufhören und mit ihm Haß und feindliches Ansehen zwischen Vater und Sohn, zwischen Bruder und Schwester. Denn sobald man die reine Lehre und Liebe Christi, wie sie ist, wird begriffen und in sich eingelebt haben, so wird man sich als Mensch groß und frei fühlen und auf ein bißchen so oder so im äussern Kultus nicht mehr sonderlichen Wert legen.

Auch werden wir alle nach und nach aus einem Christentum des Wortes und Glaubens immer mehr zu einem Christentum der Gesinnung und Tat kommen.

Frömmigkeit ist kein Zweck, sondern ein Mittel, um durch die reinste Gemütsruhe zur höchsten Kultur zu gelangen. Deswegen läßt sich bemerken, daß diejenigen, welche Frömmigkeit als Zweck und Ziel aufstecken, meistens Heuchler werden.

depths, and the human mind enlarge as it may—the sublimity and moral culture of Christianity, as it shines and glitters in the Gospels, will never be surpassed!

However, the more excellently we Protestants forge on in lofty development, the faster the Catholics will follow. As soon as they feel themselves affected by the ever increasing enlightenment of the times, they will have to fall into step, take whatever stand they may, and it will come to the point at last where all is one.

The deplorable Protestant sectarianism will come to an end, and with it the hatred and hostility between father and son, between brother and sister. For as soon as we shall have comprehended the love and teaching of Christ as they really are, and have become imbued with their spirit, we shall feel great and free as men and will no longer place such great value upon this or that in external forms of worship.

By and by we shall also emerge from a Christianity of word and creed into a Christianity of deed and conviction.

Devoutness, rather than an end, is a means for attaining the highest level of culture through purest peace of mind. Hence it may be observed that those who set up piety as an end and a goal become for the most part hypocrites.

Jesus fühlte rein und dachte
Nur den einen Gott im Stillen;
Wer ihn selbst zum Gotte machte,
Kränkte seinen heilgen Willen.

Die christliche Religion ist eine intentionierte politische Revolution, die, verfehlt, nachher moralisch geworden ist.

Wie einer ist, so ist sein Gott,
Darum ward Gott so oft zum Spott.

Da ich oft genug hatte sagen hören, jeder Mensch habe am End doch seine eigene Religion, so kam mir nichts natürlicher vor, als daß ich mir auch meine eigene bilden könne.

Ich für mich kann bei den mannigfaltigen Richtungen meines Wesens nicht an einer Denkweise genug haben. Als Dichter und Künstler bin ich Polytheist, Pantheist hingegen als Naturforscher, und eines so entschieden als das andere. Bedarf ich eines Gottes für meine Persönlichkeit, so ist dafür auch schon gesorgt. Die himmlischen und irdischen Dinge sind ein so weites Reich, daß die Organe aller Wesen zusammen es nur fassen mögen.

Wer Wissenschaft und Kunst besitzt,
Hat auch Religion;
Wer jene beiden nicht besitzt,
Der habe Religion.

Pure was Jesus in his passion,
In his heart but one God serving;
Who of him a God would fashion
From his sacred will is swerving.

The Christian religion is an abortive political revolution that turned moral.

His God each shapes as he is born,
Hence God's so oft held up to scorn.

Since I had heard often enough that everyone in the
end has his own religion, nothing seemed more
natural to me than to fashion my own.

For myself, the manifold facets of my nature make
it impossible for me to be satisfied with but a single
way of thinking. As a poet and artist I am a polytheist, while in my role as scientist I incline toward
pantheism, and both tendencies are equally marked.
When I stand in personal need of a deity, that also is
readily provided for. The things of heaven and earth
constitute so broad a realm that only the collective
organs of all creatures are able to comprehend it.

He has religion
Who has art and science;
Who has not art nor science,
Needs have religion.

Goethe as a young man
Painting by Georg May

Das Vermögen, jedes Sinnliche zu veredeln und den totesten Stoff durch Vermählung mit der geistigen Idee zu beleben, ist die sicherste Bürgschaft unsres überirdischen Ursprungs, und wie sehr wir auch durch tausend and aber tausend Erscheinungen dieser Erde angezogen und gefesselt werden, so zwingt uns doch eine innige Sehnsucht, den Blick immer wieder zum Himmel zu erheben, weil ein unerklärbares, tiefes Gefühl uns die Überzeugung gibt, daß wir Bürger jener Welten sind, die so geheimnisvoll über uns leuchten, und wir einst dahin zurückkehren werden.

The capacity for ennobling all that is sensual, of blending the utterly inanimate with the living spirit, is the surest token of our supernatural origin; and no matter how much we are drawn and shackled by a thousand and one phenomena of this earth, a resistless longing compels us ever to raise our eyes heavenward; for a deep and unfathomable sense lends us conviction that we are denizens of those worlds that so mysteriously shine above us, and that some day we shall thither return.

Die höchste Wirkung des Geistes ist, den Geist hervorzurufen.

Es ist unglaublich, wieviel der Geist zur Erhaltung des Körpers vermag. Der Geist muß nur dem Körper nicht nachgeben.

Es gibt nichts Unbedeutendes in der Welt. Es kommt nur auf die Anschauungsweise an.

Es gibt kein äußeres Zeichen der Höflichkeit, das nicht einen tiefen, sittlichen Grund hätte. Die rechte Erziehung wäre die, welche dieses Zeichen und den Grund zugleich überliefert.

Es gibt keine Lage, die man nicht veredeln könnte durch Leisten oder Dulden.

Keine Kraft geht in der Welt verloren, und nicht bloß die Seelen der Menschen sind unsterblich sondern auch alle ihre Handlungen. Sie leben fort in ihren Wirkungen.

Den Beweis der Unsterblichkeit muß jeder in sich selbst tragen, außer dem kann er nicht gegeben werden. Wohl ist alles in der Natur Wechsel, aber hinter dem Wechselnden ruht ein Ewiges.

The greatest effect of the spirit is to elicit the spirit.

It is incredible how much the mind can do to sustain the body. But the mind must not yield to the body.

There is nothing insignificant in the world. It all depends on how one looks at it.

There is no outward sign of courtesy but that has a deep moral source. A proper education would always hand down the sign together with the source.

There is no situation that cannot be ennobled by achievement or enduring.

No energy is lost in the world, nor is it merely the souls of men that are immortal but all their actions as well. They live on through their effects.

Proof of immortality each one must carry within himself—there is no other way. True, all nature is change, but behind the things that change stands something that is eternal.

Mich läßt der Gedanke an den Tod in völliger Ruhe; denn ich habe die feste Überzeugung, daß unser Geist ein Wesen ist ganz unzerstörbarer Natur, es ist ein Fortwirkendes, von Ewigkeit zu Ewigkeit, es ist der Sonne ähnlich, die bloß unsern irdischen Augen unterzugehen scheint, die aber eigentlich nie untergeht, sondern unaufhörlich leuchtet.

Die Beschäftigung mit Unsterblichkeitsideen ist für vornehme Stände und besonders für Frauenzimmer, die nichts zu tun haben. Ein tüchtiger Mensch aber, der schon hier etwas Ordentliches zu sein gedenkt und der daher täglich zu streben, zu kämpfen und zu wirken hat, läßt die künftige Welt auf sich beruhen und ist tätig und nützlich in dieser.

Ich bedaure die Menschen, welche von der Vergänglichkeit der Dinge viel Wesens machen und sich in Betrachtung irdischer Nichtigkeiten verlieren. Sind wir ja eben deshalb da, um das Vergängliche unvergänglich. machen; das kann ja nur dadurch geschehen, wenn man beides zu schätzen weiß.

Der Mensch fühlt—in allem Irdischen—doch tief und klar in sich, daß er ein Bürger jenes geistigen Reiches sei, woran wir den Glauben nicht abzulehnen noch aufzugeben vermögen. In dieser Anlehnung hegt das Geheimnis des ewigen Fortstrebens nach einem unbekannten Ziele.

The thought of death leaves me utterly unmoved; for I hold the firm conviction that our spirit is something altogether indestructible in nature, something that lives on from eon to eon, something like unto the sun, which only seems to set to our mortal eyes while indeed never setting but shining on forever.

Preoccupation with the notion of immortality is something for the leisure classes and especially for women who have nothing to do. The upright man who seeks to make something of himself here and now, hence must strive and struggle and work every day, will rest content to let the hereafter take care of itself and be active and useful in the present.

I pity people who make a great ado about the transience of things and lose themselves in contemplation of mundane trifles. We are here precisely to make the transient imperishable; and this we can do only by holding both in esteem.

Caught up in this earth, man yet feels himself deeply and clearly a denizen of that spiritual realm in which we can neither refuse nor cease to believe. This affinity holds the secret of our everlasting aspiration toward an unknown goal.

*Unsere Wünsche sind Vorgefühle der Fähig-
keiten, die in uns liegen, Vorboten desjenigen,
was wir zu leisten imstande sein werden. Was wir
können und möchten, stellt sich unserer Einbildungskraft außer uns und in der Zukunft dar; wir
fühlen eine Sehnsucht nach dem, was wir schon
im stillen besitzen. So verwandelt ein leiden-
schaftliches Vorausergreifen das wahrhaft Mögliche in ein erträumtes Wirkliche.*

Our desires presage the capacities within us; they are harbingers of what we shall be able to accomplish. What we can do and want to do is projected in our imagination, quite outside ourselves, and into the future. We are attracted to what is already ours in secret. Thus passionate anticipation transforms what is indeed possible into dreamt-for reality.

Was wir in uns nähren, das wächst, das ist ein ewiges Naturgesetz.

Von Natur besitzen wir keinen Fehler, der nicht zur Tugend, keine Tugend, die nicht zum Fehler werden könnte.

Vollkommenheit ist die Norm des Himmels, Vollkommenes wollen die Norm des Menschen.

Der Tag gehört dem Irrtum und dem Fehler, die Zeitreihe dem Erfolg und dem Gelingen.

Wir bekennen uns zu dem Geschlecht, das aus dem Dunkeln ins Helle strebt.

Es sind nur wenige, die den Sinn haben und zugleich zur Tat fähig sind. Der Sinn erweitert, aber lähmt; die·Tat belebt, aber beschränkt.

Der Handelnde is immer gewissenlos; es hat niemand Gewissen als der Betrachtende.

Handeln ist leicht, Denken schwer, nach dem Gedachten handeln unbequem.

Es ist nichts schrecklicher als eine tätige Unwissenheit.

What we nourish within ourselves grows—such is the everlasting law of nature.

As we are constituted by nature, there is not a fault that could not turn into a virtue, no virtue that could not turn into a fault.

Perfection is the norm of heaven, the pursuit of perfection that of man.

The passing day is prey to error. Time commands success and achievement.

We profess our allegiance to that kinship which strives from darkness toward light.

But few have comprehension and are at once capable of action. Comprehension expands but paralyzes; action inspires but limits.

While acting a man is without conscience. He can have a conscience only when he reflects.

To act is easy, to think difficult, to act in keeping with thought irksome.

Nothing is worse than active ignorance.

Der Mensch muß bei dem Glauben verharren, daß das Unbegreifliche begreiflich sei, er würde sonst nicht forschen.

Niemand, wenn er auch noch soviel besitzt, kann ohne Sehnsucht bestehen, die wahre Sehnsucht aber muß gegen ein Unerreichbares gerichtet sein.

Man must cling to his faith that the incomprehensible is comprehensible, else he would cease to investigate.

No man, however much he may possess, can live on without longing; true longing must be directed toward the unattainable.

Gott gibt die Nüsse, aber er bricht sie nicht auf.

God gave us the nuts, but he will not crack them for us.

Jeder hat sein eigen Glück unter den Händen, wie der Künstler eine rohe Materie, die er zu einer Gestalt umbilden will. Aber es ist mit dieser Kunst wie mit allen: nur die Fähigkeit dazu wird uns angeboren, sie will gelernt und sorgfältig ausgeübt sein.

Das Muß ist hart, aber beim Muß kann der Mensch allein zeigen, wie's inwendig um ihn steht. Willkürlich leben kann jeder.

Wie kann man sich selbst kennenlernen? Durch Betrachten niemals, wohl aber durch Handeln. Versuche deine Pflicht zu tun, und du weißt gleich, was an dir ist.

Allem Leben, allem Tun, aller Kunst muß das Handwerk vorausgehen, welches nur in der Beschränkung erworben wird. Eines recht wissen und ausüben, gibt höhere Bildung, als Halbheit im Hundertfältigen.

Vergebens werden ungebundene Geister
Nach der Vollendung reiner Höhe streben.
Wer Großes will, muß sich zusammenraffen.
In der Beschränkung zeigt sich erst der Meister
Und das Gesetz nur kann uns Freiheit geben.

Bei dem größten Verlust müssen wir sogleich umherschauen, was uns zu erhalten und zu leisten übrig bleibt.

Each has his own happiness in his hands, as the artist handles the rude clay he seeks to reshape into a figure; yet it is the same with this art as with all others: only the capacity for it is innate; the art itself must be learned and painstakingly practiced.

Coercion is harsh, but only under compulsion do men show what is in them. Everyone can manage when he is free to do as he pleases.

How may one get to know oneself? Never by contemplation, only, indeed, by action. Seek to do your duty, and you will know at once how it is with you.

Before all life, all work, all art must come the work of the hand, skill in which is acquired but in a restricted compass. To know and practice a craft lends greater culture than half knowledge a hundred times over.

It is in vain when talent loath of bridle
Tries to attain the crown of full perfection.
He who aims high must gladly brook the harness:
To prove himself the master needs restriction,
And rule alone can give a man his freedom.

In the face of even the greatest loss we must instantly review what is left to us, and what is left to us to do.

Laß nur die Sorge sein,
Das gibt sich alles schon,
Und fällt der Himmel ein,
Kommt doch eine Lerche davon.

Die Vorsehung hat tausend Mittel, die Gefallenen zu
erheben und die Niedergebeugten aufzurichten.
Manchmal sieht unser Schicksal aus wie ein Frucht-
baum im Winter. Wer sollte bei dem traurigen An-
sehn desselben wohl denken, daß diese starren Äste,
diese zackigen Zweige im nächsten Frühjahr wieder
grünen, blühen, sodann Früchte tragen könnten;
doch wir hoffens, wir wissens.

Schaff, das Tagwerk meiner Hände,
Hohes Glück, daß ich's vollende!
Laß, o laß mich nicht ermatten!
Nein, es sind nicht leere Träume:
Jetzt nur Stangen, diese Bäume
Geben einst noch Frucht und Schatten.

Noch ist es Tag, da rühre sich der Mann,
Die Nacht tritt ein, wo niemand wirken kann.

Das Tagwerk, das mir aufgetragen ist, das mir
täglich leichter und schwerer wird, erfordert wa-
chend und träumend meine Gegenwart. Diese Pflicht
wird mir täglich teurer und darin wünscht' ich's den
größten Menschen gleich zu tun, und in nichts
Größerem. Diese Begierde, die Pyramide meines
Lebens, deren Basis mis angegeben und begründet
ist, so hoch als möglich in die Luft zu spitzen, über-

Forsake your worries all—
You have come through many a scrape—
And should the heavens fall,
One lark is sure to escape.

Providence has a thousand means to raise the fallen
and lift up the prostrate. Sometimes our fate resem-
bles a fruit tree in winter. Who would think at be-
holding such a sad sight that those rigid branches,
those jagged twigs will turn green again in the spring
and blossom and bear fruit, but we hope it, we
know it.

Give me—bliss of daily striving,
Give me trust it will be thriving!
Keep my strength, keep it from fading!
No, it is not idle dreaming:
Spindly stalks these trees now seeming ˙
Will in time give fruit and shading.

Day is not past, let none his labor shirk;
Night comes, when none can do his work.

The work with which I am charged grows easier
and at once harder day by day, requiring my presence, awake or asleep. These duties I cherish more
and more every day, and in their performance—and
nothing beyond that—I could wish to equal the
greatest men. This craving to rear up into the air as
high as possible the pyramid of my life, the base of
which has been given and established for me, out-

wiegt alles andere und läßt kaum augenblickliches Vergessen zu. Ich darf mich nicht säumen, ich bin schon weit in Jahren vor, und vielleicht bricht mich das Schicksal in der Mitte, und der babylonische Turm bleibt stumpf und unvollendet. Wenigstens soll man sagen, er war kühn entworfen, und wenn ich lebe, sollen, will's Gott, die Kräfte bis hinauf reichen.

Wenn man einmal weiß, worauf alles ankommt, hört man auf, gesprächig zu sein. Worauf kommt nun alles an? Das ist bald gesagt: Denken und Tun, Tun und Denken, das ist die Summe aller Weisheit. . . . Beides muß wie Aus- und Einatmen sich im Leben ewig fort hin und wieder bewegen. Wer sich zum Gesetz macht, das Tun am Denken, das Denken am Tun zu prüfen, der kann nicht irren, und irrt er, so wird er sich bald auf den rechten Weg zurückfinden.

Daß mein Denken sich von den Gegenständen nicht sondere . . . daß mein Anschauen selbst ein Denken, mein Denken ein Anschauen sei.

Es ist besser, das geringste Ding von der Welt zu tun, als eine halbe Stunde für zu gering halten.

Ihrer sechzig hat die Stunde.
Über tausend hat der Tag.
Söhnchen! werde dir die Kunde
Was man alles leisten mag.

weighs all else and scarcely permits of even a momentary lapse. I must not flag, for I am already advanced in years and fate may halt me in my tracks, with my Tower of Babylon uncapped and incomplete. Let them at least say that it was bold in design; and if, God willing, I live on, my powers shall reach to the top.

Once one knows what really matters, one ceases to be voluble. And what does really matter? That is easy: thinking and doing, doing and thinking—these are the sum of all wisdom. . ... Both must move ever onward in life, to and fro, like breathing in and breathing out. Whoever makes it a rule to test action by thought, thought by action, cannot falter, and if he does, will soon find his way back to the right road.

That my perception be not separated from things . . . that my perception itself be thinking, my thinking perception.

It is better to do the smallest thing in the world than to hold half an hour to be too small a thing.

Sixty are in every hour.
Fourteen-forty in a day.
Each one, son, provides some power
To achieve or flit away.

Etwas muß getan sein in jedem Moment, und wie wollt' es geschehen, achtete man nicht auf das Werk wie auf die Stunde?

Was aber ist deine Pflicht? Die Forderung des Tages.

Something must be accomplished every moment of the day, and how could this be done unless one paid attention to both the work and the clock?

And just what is your duty? The demands of the day.

Es ist nichts groß als das Wahre, und das kleinste Wahre ist groß. Ich kam neulich auf einen Gedanken, der mich sagen ließ: Auch eine schädliche Wahrheit ist nützlich, weil sie nur Augenblicke schädlich sein kann und alsdann zu anderen Wahrheiten führt, die immer nützlicher und sehr nützlich werden müssen, und umgekehrt ist ein nützlicher Irrtum schädlich, weil er es nur augenblicklich sein kann und in andere Irrtümer verleitet, die immer schädlicher werden.

Nothing is great but truth, and the smallest aspect of the true is great. The other day I had a thought, which I formulated like this: Even a harmful truth is useful, for it can be harmful only for the moment and will lead to other truths, which must always become more and more useful. Conversely, even a useful untruth is harmful, for it can be useful only for the moment, leading us into other untruths, which become more and more harmful.

Zum Ergreifen der Wahrheit braucht es ein viel höheres Organ als zur Verteidigung des Irrtums.

Man muß das Wahre immer wiederholen, weil auch der Irrtum um uns her immer wieder gepredigt wird, und zwar nicht von Einzelnen, sondern von der Masse.

Das Wahre ist eine Fackel, aber eine ungeheure; deswegen suchen wir alle nur blinzelnd so daran vorbei zu kommen, in Furcht sogar, uns zu verbrennen.

Es ist nicht immer nötig, daß das Wahre sich verkörpere, schon genug, wenn es geistig umherschwebt und Übereinstimmung bewirkt, wenn es wie Glokkenton ernst-freundlich durch die Lüfte wogt.

Nie verläßt uns der Irrtum, doch ziehet ein höher Bedürfnis
Immer den strebenden Geist leise zur Wahrheit hinan.

Das Wahre, mit dem Göttlichen identisch, läßt sich niemals direkt von uns erkennen: wir schauen es nur im Abglanz, im Beispiel, Symbol, in einzelnen und verwandten Erscheinungen.

Truth is like a torch, but of gigantic proportions. That is why we hurry past it with dazzled eyes in fear of even getting scorched.

One must ever repeat what is true because error, too, is always preached around us, and this not by the few but by the many.

It requires a much higher sensitivity to seize upon truth than to defend error.

It is not always necessary for truth to take on concrete form. Its spiritual presence, like the grave and friendly peal of a bell trembling in the air, is quite sufficient to bring about accord.

Never will error release us, but always transcendent endeavor
Leads on the mind which persists, nearer—most gently—to truth.

We can never directly recognize truth, which is identical with the divine. We see it but by reflection, example, symbol—in single or related phenomena.

Man kann das Gewissen belügen, aber nicht täuschen.

Man wird nie betrogen, man betrügt sich selbst.

Der törigste von allen Irrtümern ist, wenn junge gute Köpfe glauben, ihre Originalität zu verlieren, indem sie das Wahre anerkennen, was von andern schon anerkannt worden.

Eine nachgesprochene Wahrheit verliert schon ihre Grazie, aber ein nachgesprochener Irrtum ist ganz ekelhaft.

Die Menschen verdrießt's, daß das Wahre so einfach ist; sie sollten bedenken, daß sie noch Mühe genug haben, es praktisch zu ihrem Nutzen anzuwenden.

Was fruchtbar ist, allein ist wahr.

One can lie to one's conscience, but one cannot deceive it.

We are never deceived—we deceive ourselves.

Most foolish of all errors is when bright young minds believe they will forfeit their originality by acknowledging as true what others have already so acknowledged.

Truth parroted loses all its grace, but error parroted is a complete abomination.

Man is irked that truth is so simple. Let him consider how troublesome it is to turn truth to his profit in practice.

That alone is true which is fruitful.

Das fruchtbarste Lernen ist die Überwindung des eigenen Irrtums. Wer keinen Irrtum eingestehen will, kann ein großer Gelehrter sein, aber er ist kein großer Lerner. Wer sich des Irrtums schämt, der sträubt sich, ihn zu erkennen und zuzugeben, das heißt, er sträubt sich vor seinem besten innerlichen Gewinn.

The most fruitful lesson is the conquest of one's own error. Whoever refuses to admit error may be a great scholar, but he is not a great learner. Whoever is ashamed of error will struggle against recognizing and admitting it, which means that he struggles against his greatest inward gain.

Da jedermann irrt, da die Weisesten geirrt haben, so haben wir keinen Grund, unsern Irrtum als etwas Schändliches zu empfinden.

Nur durch Fehler, die einen recht ärgern, rückt man fort.

Nicht vor Irrtum zu bewahren, ist die Pflicht des Menschenerziehers; sondern den Irrenden zu leiten, ja ihn seinen Irrtum aus vollen Bechern ausschlürfen zu lassen, das ist Weisheit der Lehrer. Wer seinen Irrtum nur kostet, hält lange damit haus; er freut sich dessen, als eines seltenen Glücks; aber wer ihn ganz erschöpft, der muß ihn kennenlernen, wenn er nicht wahnsinnig ist.

Die Mängel aufdecken ist nicht genug; ja man hat unrecht, solches zu tun, wenn man nicht zugleich das Mittel zu dem besseren Zustande anzugeben weiß.

Es ist Pflicht, andern nur dasjenige zu sagen, was sie aufnehmen können. Der Mensch versteht nichts, als was ihm gemäß ist.

Wenn wir die Menschen nur nehmen, wie sie sind, so machen wir sie schlechter; wenn wir sie behandeln, als wären sie, was sie sein sollten, so bringen wir sie dahin, wohin sie zu bringen sind.

Since everyone errs, since the wisest have erred, we have no ground for regarding our own errors as shameful.

Only by errors that really irk us do we advance.

The educator's task is not to preserve from error but rather to guide the errant; indeed, to let them savor their errors to the dregs—such is the teacher's wisdom. Whoever barely tastes his error will long nurse it, will revel in it as though in a rare treat; but whoever drains it to the bottom must come to know it, unless he be mad.

To uncover deficiencies is not enough; indeed, it is wrong to do so, unless one knows and cites the means for improvement.

It is our duty to tell others but what they are able to receive. Man grasps but what is to his measure.

If we take people but as they are, we make them worse; if we treat them as though they were what they should be, we bring them whither they should be brought.

Was man nicht versteht, besitzt man nicht.

Alles Verständnis fängt mit Bewunderung an.

Man lernt nichts kennen, als was man liebt, und je
tiefer und vollständiger die Kenntnis werden soll,
desto stärker, kräftiger und lebendiger muß Liebe,
ja Leidenschaft sein.

Liebe und Not sind doch die besten Meister.

We cannot make our own what we do not understand.

All understanding begins with admiration.

One learns to know only what one loves, and the deeper and fuller the knowledge is to be, the more powerful and vivid must be the love, indeed, the passion.

Love and necessity are still the best taskmasters.

Jedem Alter des Menschen antwortet eine gewisse Philosophie. Das Kind erscheint als Realist; denn es findet sich so überzeugt von dem Dasein der Birnen und Äpfel als von dem seinigen. Der Jüngling, von inneren Leidenschaften bestürmt, muß auf sich selbst merken, sich vorfühlen, er wird zum Idealisten umgewandelt. Dagegen ein Skeptiker zu sein, hat der Mann alle Ursache; er tut wohl, zu zweifeln, ob das Mittel, das er zum Zwecke gewählt hat, auch das rechte sei. Vor dem Handeln, im Handeln hat er alle Ursache, den Verstand beweglich zu erhalten, damit er nicht nachher sich über ein falsche Wahl zu betrüben habe. Der Greis jedoch wird sich immer zum Mystizismus bekennen, er sieht, daß so vieles vom Zufall abzuhängen scheint, das Unvernünftige gelingt, das Vernünftige schlägt fehl, Glück und Unglück stellen sich unerwartet ins Gleiche; so ist es, so war es, und das hohe Alter beruhigt sich in dem, der da ist, der da war und der da sein wird.

Every age of man accords with a certain philosophy. The child appears a realist; for he finds himself as convinced of the existence of apples and pears as of his own. The youth, assailed by inward passions, must listen to himself, grope his way; he becomes transformed into an idealist. The man has every reason to be a skeptic; he does well to doubt whether the means to an end he has chosen is right. Before action, in action he has every reason to keep his mind nimble lest he later repent of a wrong choice. The elder will ever profess mysticism; he sees so much seemingly depending on chance, unreason prevailing, reason failing, good fortune and ill unexpectedly in balance. Thus it is, thus it was; and great age comes to rest within Him who is, was and will be.

Wenn auch die Welt im ganzen vorschreitet, die Jugend muß doch immer wieder von vorn anfangen und als Individuum die Epochen der Weltkultur durchmachen.

Beim Kleinen beginnt alles, und je größer und mächtiger etwas werden soll, desto langsamer und scheinbar mühsamer wächst es.

Ein Blatt, das groß werden soll, ist voller Runzeln und Knittern, eh es sich entwickelt; wenn man nun nicht Geduld hat und es gleich so glatt haben will wie ein Weidenblatt, dann ist's übel.

Wir sollen es mit den Kindern machen, wie Gott mit uns, der uns am glücklichsten macht, wenn er uns im freundlichen Wahn so hintaumeln läßt.

Denn wir können die Kinder nach unserem Sinne
   nicht formen;
So wie Gott sie uns gab, so muß man sie haben und
   lieben,
Sie erziehen aufs beste und jeglichen lassen
   gewähren.

Man liebt an dem Mädchen, was es ist, und an dem Jüngling, was er ankündigt.

The world as a whole moves onward, but youth must begin ever anew, individually reliving all the epochs of world culture.

Everything begins little, and the greater and mightier it is to become, the slower it seems to grow and the more difficult its growth appears.

A leaf that is destined to grow large is full of grooves and wrinkles before it develops. Now if one has no patience and wants it smooth like a willow leaf, there is trouble ahead.

We should do with children as God does with us. He makes us happiest when he allows us to totter on ahead in our pleasurable illusions.

Children can scarcely be fashioned to meet with our
    likes and our purpose.
Just as God did us give them, so must we hold
    them and love them,
Nurture and teach them to fullness and leave them
    to be what they are.

We love a girl for what she is and a youth for what he promises to be.

Wahrlich, die Jugend wäre unerträglich, wär ich nicht auch einmal unerträglich gewesen.

Der Irrtum ist recht gut, solange wir jung sind; man muß ihn nur nicht mit ins Alter schleppen.

Wer in einem gewissen Alter frühere Jugendwünsche und Hoffnungen realisieren will, betrügt sich immer, denn jedes Jahrzehnt des Menschen hat sein eigenes Glück, seine Hoffnungen und Aussichten. Wehe dem Menschen, der vorwärts oder rückwärts zu greifen durch Umstände oder Wahn veranlaßt wird!

Das Alter ist ein höflich Mann
Einmal übers andere klopft er an;
Aber nun sagt niemand: Herein!
Und vor der Tür will er nicht sein.
Da klinkt er auf, tritt ein so schnell,
Und nun heißts, er sei ein grober Gesell.

Wenn man alt ist, muß man mehr tun, als da man jung war.

Kein Segen kommt der Arbeit gleich, und nur der Mensch, welcher sein Leben lang gearbeitet hat, kann sagen: ich habe gelebt.

Young people would indeed be intolerable—but for the fact that I myself was once intolerable.

Error is all right so long as we are young, but we must not carry it into our old age.

Whoever at a given age seeks to realize hopes and desires of his earlier years is doomed to deceive himself; for man's every decade holds its own share of happiness, its own hopes and prospects. Woe unto the man whom delusion or circumstance persuade to reach forward or backward!

Age is a very courteous chap.
Knocks on the door with many a wrap.
But bid him in no one does care.
And since he finds it cold out there,
At length he slips in quick and sure.
And now we call him a beastly boor.

When one is old one must do more than when one was young.

No blessing is equal to the blessings of work. Only life-long work entitles a man to say: I have lived.

Man darf nur alt werden, um milder zu sein; ich sehe keinen Fehler begehen, den ich nicht auch begangen hätte..

In der Jugend, wo wir nichts besitzen oder doch ruhigen Besitz nicht zu schätzen wissen, sind wir Demokraten; sind wir aber in einem langen Leben zu Eigentum gekommen, so wünschen wir dieses nicht allein gesichert, sondern wir wünschen auch, daß unsere Kinder und Enkel das Erworbene ruhig genießen mögen. Deshalb sind wir im Alter immer Aristokraten ohne Ausnahme, wenn wir auch in der Jugend uns zu anderen Gesinnungen hinneigten.

Wir erfahren erst im Alter, was uns in der Jugend begegnete.

Der ist der glücklichste Mensch, der das Ende seines Lebens mit dem Anfang in Verbindung setzen kann.

Ist nicht das Leben kurz genug? Sollen die sich nicht anfassen, deren Weg miteinander geht?

When a man grows old, he should become mellow. I see no wrong committed which I might not have committed myself.

In our youth, when we possess nothing, or at least do not appreciate quiet possession, we are democrats. But when in the course of a long life we have come to acquire property, we wish this not only to be secure but also that our children and grandchildren may have the undisturbed enjoyment of what we have acquired. Therefore in old age we are aristocrats, without exception, even if we leaned toward different sentiments in our youth.

We learn only in old age what happened to us in our youth.

He is the happiest who can integrate the end of his life with its beginnings.

Is not life short enough? Should we not join hands with those who go our way?

Grand Duke Karl August von Sachsen-Weimar
Painting by Wilhelm Tischbein

Willst du dich selber erkennen, so sieh, wie die
andern es treiben;
Willst du die andern verstehn, blick in dein ei-
genes Herz.

*If knowing yourself is your purpose, just watch
what your neighbors are doing.
Knowledge of others you gain, probing within
yourself.*

Alles Behagen am Leben ist auf eine regelmäßige Wiederkehr der äußeren Dinge gegründet. Der Wechsel von Tag und Nacht, der Jahreszeiten, der Blüten und Früchte, und was sonst von Epoche zu Epoche entgegentritt, damit wir es genießen können und sollen, diese sind die eigentlichen Triebfedern des irdischen Lebens. Je offner wir für diese Genüsse sind, desto glücklicher fühlen wir uns.

Der Mensch mache sich nur irgendeine würdige Gewohnheit zu eigen, an der er sich die Lust in heiteren Tagen erhöhen und in trüben Tagen aufrichten kann. Er gewöhne sich zum Beispiel, täglich in der Bibel oder im Homer zu lesen, oder Medaillen oder schöne Bilder zu schauen, oder gute Musik zu hören. Aber es muß etwas Treffliches, Würdiges sein, woran er sich so gewöhnt, damit ihm stets und in jeder Lage der Respekt dafür bleibe.

In der Gewohnheit ruht das einzige Behagen des Menschen; selbst das Unangenehme, woran wir uns gewöhnten, vermissen wir ungern.

Wie wenig der Mensch bedarf, und wie lieb es ihm wird, wenn er fühlt, wie sehr er das Wenige bedarf!

Man muß nur in die Fremde gehen, um das Gute kennenzulernen, was man zu Hause besitzt.

All enjoyment of pleasure in living is grounded in the regular recurrence of outward things. The alternation of day and night, of the seasons, of bloom and fruit —and whatever else is ours to enjoy down the cycle of time—these are the true mainsprings of life. The more openly we avow these pleasures, the happier we are.

Let man but acquire some worthy habit, to enhance his pleasure on fine days and succor him on the bad. Let him, for example, read the Bible every day, or Homer, or contemplate medallions or fine pictures, or listen to good music. It must, however, be something of excellence and worth, to which he becomes so inured—that his respect for it never fail, in any circumstance.

Habit is man's sole comfort. We dislike doing without even unpleasant things to which we have become used.

How little man needs, and how comforting it is, when he realizes how much he needs that little!

One needs only to go abroad to learn to appreciate what one has at home.

Das sicherste Mittel, ein freundliches Verhältnis zu hegen und zu pflegen, finde ich darin, daß man sich wechselweise mitteile, was man tut; denn die Menschen treffen vielmehr zusammen in dem, was sie tun, als in dem, was sie denken.

Die Menschen werden durch Gesinnungen geeinigt, durch Meinungen getrennt.

So viele widersetzen sich dem Echten nur deshalb, weil sie zugrunde gehen würden, wenn sie es anerkennten.

Wir gestehen lieber unsre moralischen Irrtümer, Fehler und Gebrechen als unsre wissenschaftlichen. . . . Das kommt daher, weil das Gewissen demütig ist und sich sogar in der Beschämung gefällt; der Verstand aber ist hochmütig, und ein abgenötigter Widerruf bringt ihn in Verzweiflung.

Wenn einer nur das Schöne, der andere nur das Nützliche befördert, so machen beide zusammen erst einen Menschen aus.

Durch nichts bezeichnen die Menschen mehr ihren Charakter als durch das, was sie lächerlich finden.

Toren und gescheite Leute sind gleich unschädlich. Nur die Halbnarren und die Halbweisen, das sind die gefährlichsten.

The surest way to cultivate and preserve a friendly relation is to communicate to each other what we are doing; for people are much more likely to agree in what they do than in what they think.

Men are united by sentiment, separated by opinion.

So many people resist acknowledging reality only because they would perish if they accepted it.

We would rather admit our moral errors, faults and foibles than our scientific ones. . . . This is because conscience is humble and even pleased with its own humility; while reason is arrogant, being driven to despair when forced to recant.

If the one further but the beautiful, another but the useful, only the two together will make up a man.

Through nothing do people reveal their character more than by what they laugh about.

Fools and wise men are equally harmless. It is the half-fools and the half-wise who are the most dangerous.

Allgemeine Begriffe und großer Dünkel sind immer auf dem Wege, entsetzliches Unglück anzurichten.

Armer Mensch, an dem der Kopf alles ist.

Man kann einen Vorsatz nicht sicherer abstumpfen, als wenn man ihn öfters durchspricht.

Man darf keinen Zustand, der länger dauern, ja, der eigentlich ein Beruf, eine Lebensweise werden soll, mit einer Feierlichkeit anfangen. Man feiere nur, was glücklich vollendet ist. Alle Zeremonien zum Anfange erschöpfen Lust und Kräfte, die das Streben hervorbringen und uns bei einer fortgesetzten Mühe beistehen sollen. Unter allen Festen ist das Hochzeitsfest das unschicklichste; keines sollte mehr in Stille, Demut und Hoffnung begangen werden als dieses.

Willst du ins Unendliche schreiten,
Geh nur im Endlichen nach allen Seiten.

Wir lernen die Menschen nicht kennen, wenn sie zu uns kommen; wir müssen zu ihnen gehen, um zu erfahren, wie es mit ihnen steht.

Mann mit zugeknöpften Taschen,
Dir tut niemand was zu lieb:
Hand wird nur von Hand gewaschen;
Wenn du nehmen willst, so gib!

Fixed concepts and great conceit are always ready to wreak dreadful havoc.

Poor fellow who is all head!

There is no surer way to blunt a resolution than to keep talking about it.

No state that is to endure, that is, indeed, to be a vocation, a way of life, should begin with solemnities. Celebrate but what is well done. All ceremony at the outset but drains will and strength that should give rise to striving and aid us in sustained effort. Among all festivals wedding celebrations are the unseemliest. None stand in greater need of being observed with hope, humility and reticence.

Wilt thou into infinities wander,
Roam through the finite hither and yonder!

We do not learn to know men by their coming to us.
We must go to them to find out what they are like.

Button not thy pockets, brother,
None will thee a kindness give;
One hand's washed but by another,
Thou must give, wouldst thou receive!

Sage nicht, daß du geben willst, sondern gib! Die Hoffnung befriedigst du nie.

Man würde viel Almosen geben, wenn man Augen hätte zu sehen, was eine empfangende Hand für ein schönes Bild macht.

Bequemer ist es freilich, die Welt nach der Idee zu modeln, als seine Vorstellungen den Dingen zu unterwerfen.

Es ist keine Kunst, geistreich zu sein, wenn man vor nichts Respekt hat.

Der Mensch kann nicht lange im bewußten Zustande oder im Bewußtsein verharren, er muß sich wieder ins Unbewußte flüchten, denn darin lebt seine Wurzel.

Der Mensch mag sich wenden, wohin er will, er mag unternehmen, was es auch sei, stets wird er auf jenen Weg wieder zurückkehren, den ihm die Natur einmal vorgezeichnet hat.

Der Mensch ist nicht eher glücklich, als bis sein unbedingtes Streben sich selbst seine Begrenzung bestimmt.

Never say you will give, but give! You will never live up to hopes.

We would give alms generously, if we had eyes to see the beauty in the picture of an accepting hand.

True, it is easier to fashion the world after the idea than to subject one's notions to things.

When one respects nothing, it is no trick to be brilliant.

Man cannot long endure the state of awareness or consciousness. He must ever again escape into the unconscious, for there live his roots.

Man may twist and turn, do what he will, he must ever return to the path nature has once for all prescribed for him.

Man will not rest until his limitless striving sets itself its own limitations.

Hypothesen sind Wiegenlieder, womit der Lehrer seine Schüler einlullt; der denkende treue Beobachter lernt immer mehr seine Beschränkung kennen; er sieht, je weiter sich das Wissen ausbreitet, desto mehr Probleme kommen zum Vorschein.

Je weiter man in der Erfahrung fortrückt, desto näher kommt man dem Unerforschlichen; je mehr man die Erfahrung zu nutzen weiß, desto mehr sieht man, daß das Unerforschliche keinen praktischen Nutzen hat.

Hypotheses are lullabies for teachers to sing their students to sleep. The close and thoughtful observer more and more learns to recognize his limitations. He realizes that with the steady growth of knowledge more and more new problems keep on emerging.

The further one advances in experience, the closer one comes to the unfathomable; the more one learns to utilize experience, the more one recognizes that the unfathomable is of no practical value.

Willst du dich deines Wertes freuen,
So mußt der Welt du Wert verleihen.

If thine own value thou wouldst relish
The world with worth thou must embellish.

Große Gedanken und ein reines Herz, das ist, was wir von Gott erbitten sollen.

Ohne Ernst ist in der Welt nichts möglich, und unter denen, die wir gebildete Menschen nennen, ist eigentlich wenig Ernst zu finden; sie gehen gegen Arbeit und Geschäfte, gegen Künste, ja, gegen Vergnügungen nur mit einer Art von Selbstverteidigung zu Werke; man lebt, wie man ein Pack Zeitungen liest, nur damit man sie loswerde. Man will mancherlei wissen und kennen, und gerade das, was einen am wenigsten angeht, und man bemerkt nicht, daß kein Hunger dadurch gestillt wird, wenn man nach der Luft schnappt. Wenn ich einen Menschen kennen lerne, frage ich sogleich: womit beschäftigt er sich? und wie? und in welcher Folge? und mit der Beantwortung der Frage ist auch mein Interesse an ihm zeitlebens entschieden.

Was die Einsamkeit betrifft, so kann ich nicht begreifen, wie gewisse Leute Anspruch auf Geistesbildung oder auf Seelengröße und Charakter machen wollen, und doch nicht das mindeste Gefühl für das Alleinsein haben. Denn die Einsamkeit verbunden mit dem ruhigen Anschauen der Natur, mit einem klaren, heiteren Bewußtsein seines Glaubens über Schöpfung und Schöpfer, und verbunden mit einigen Widerwärtigkeiten von außen, ist, ich behaupte es, die einzige wahre Schule für einen Geist von edlen Anlagen; und wer nicht seine schönsten Träume in

Great thoughts and a pure heart—that is what we ought to pray to God for.

Without serious intent nothing is possible in this world, yet among those we call educated we find few who take things seriously. They tackle work and business, art and even amusement but with a kind of defensivenes. We live as we read a stack of newspapers, just to be rid of them. We seek to know many things, for the most part what concerns us least, and we fail to note that hunger is not appeased by snapping at the empty air. Whenever I meet someone, I ask at once: What does he do? How? In what sequence? And the reply determines my interest in him for all time.

As for solitude, I cannot understand how certain people seek to lay claim to intellectual stature, nobility of soul and strength of character, yet have not the slightest feeling for seclusion; for solitude, I maintain, when joined with a quiet contemplation of nature, a serene and conscious faith in creation and the Creator, and a few vexations from outside is the only true school for a mind of lofty endowment. Unless one dream one's finest dreams in solitude,

der Einsamkeit träumt, wer nicht so weit gekommen ist, daß er jede menschliche Gesellschaft, alle Zerstreuungen und allen Umgang mit der Welt, ja sogar den Umgang mit großen Seelen und wirklich guten Gemütern entbehren kann, wer sich nicht selbst genug, wer nicht die erste und beste Unterhaltung in sich selbst, in der Tiefe seines eigenen Ichs findet, der schiebe seine Ansprüche auf Geistesgröße bescheidentlich in die Tasche zu den übrigen Brotkrumen und Bettelmünzen, die dort befindlich sind, und schleiche sich fort aus dem Angesicht der heiligen Natur, der er doch nicht angehört.

Man verliert nicht immer, wenn man entbehrt.

Sich in seiner Beschränktheit gefallen, ist ein elender Zustand; in Gegenwart des Besten seine Beschränktheit fühlen, ist freilich ängstlich, aber diese Angst erhebt.

Es gibt kein Vergangenes, das man zurücksehnen dürfte, es gibt nur ein ewig Neues, das sich aus den erweiterten Elementen des Vergangenen gestaltet, und die echte Sehnsucht muß stets produktiv sein, ein Neues, Besseres erschaffen.

Das Gleiche läßt uns in Ruhe; aber der Widerspruch ist es, der uns produktiv macht.

unless one reach the point of being able to dispense with all human company, all distraction, all traffic with the world—even the companionship of great souls and first-rate minds—unless one be self-sufficient, finding the first and best entertainment within oneself, within the depth of one's own person, one ought to sweep one's claims to greatness into one's pocket with the other bread crumbs and almoners' pence there accumulated, one ought to steal away out of the sacred presence of a nature to which one does not belong.

One does not always lose if he has to do without.

To be pleased with one's limitations is a wretched state. To sense one's limitations in the presence of a better is disconcerting, but the resultant anxiety can serve to inspire the mind.

There is nothing in the past that one should wish back. There is only the ever new, taking shape from the expanded elements of the past; and true nostalgia must always be productive, creating something new and better.

The like leaves us unmoved; it is contradiction that makes us productive.

Die Welt kann nur durch die gefördert werden, die sich ihr entgegensetzen.

Die große Notwendigkeit erhebt, die kleine erniedrigt den Menschen.

Alle Epochen, in welchen der Glaube * herrscht, unter welcher Gestalt er auch wolle, sind glänzend, herzerhebend und fruchtbar für Mitwelt und Nachwelt.

Was man mündlich ausspricht, muß der Gegenwart, dem Augenblick gewidmet sein; was man schreibt, widme man der Ferne, der Folge.

Man säe nur, man erntet mit der Zeit.

* Nicht dogmatischer Kirchenglaube ist hier gemeint, sondern der Glaube an das Grosse und Gute im Menschen.

The world advances only because of those who oppose it.

Great necessity elevates man, petty necessity casts him down.

All epochs in history dominated by faith,* under whatever guise, are brilliant, inspiring and fruitful for those who live in them as well as for posterity.

What one says should be addressed to the present, the moment; what one writes, to the future, to posterity.

But sow, and you will reap in time.

---

* Dogmatic church belief is not meant here, but rather the belief in man's capacity for the great and good.

Volk und Knecht und Überwinder,
Sie gestehn zu jeder Zeit:
Höchstes Glück der Erdenkinder
Sei nur die Persönlichkeit.

Jedes Leben sei zu führen,
Wenn man sich nicht selbst vermißt;
Alles könne man verlieren,
Wenn man bliebe, was man ist.

Those in bondage, those in power,
All men of all times agree
That creation's highest flower
Is man's personality,

That no life deserves man's scorning
If he, what he is, remains,
That no loss is worth his mourning
If his self he but retains.

Man hat mich immer als einen vom Glück besonders Begünstigten gepriesen; auch will ich mich nicht beklagen und den Gang meines Lebens nicht schelten. Allein, im Grunde ist es nichts als Mühe und Arbeit gewesen, und ich kann wohl sagen, daß ich in meinen fünfundsiebzig Jahren keine vier Wochen eigentliches Behagen gehabt. . . . Mein eigentliches Glück war mein poetisches Sinnen und Schaffen. . . . Ein weitverbreiteter Name, eine hohe Stellung im Leben sind gute Dinge. Allein mit all meinem Namen und Stande habe ich es nicht weiter gebracht, als daß ich, um nicht zu verletzen, zu der Meinung anderer schweige.

Nun heißt es wieder, ich sei ein Fürstendiener, ich sei ein Fürstenknecht. Als ob damit etwas gesagt wäre! Diene ich denn etwa einem Tyrannen? einem Despoten? Diene ich denn etwa einem solchen, der auf Kosten des Volkes nur seinen eigenen Lüsten lebt? Solche Fürsten und solche Zeiten liegen gottlob längst hinter uns. Ich bin dem Großherzog seit einem halben Jahrhundert auf das innigste verbunden und habe ein halbes Jahrhundert mit ihm gestrebt und gearbeitet; aber lügen müßte ich, wenn ich sagen sollte, ich wüßte einen einzigen Tag, wo der Großherzog nicht daran gedacht hätte, etwas zu tun und auszuführen, das dem Lande zum Wohle gereichte, und das geeignet wäre, den Zustand des einzelnen zu verbessern. Für sich persönlich, was hatte er denn von seinem Fürstenstande als Last und Mühe! Ist seine Wohnung, seine Kleidung und seine Tafel etwa

I have always been held up as one whom fortune especially favored; nor do I mean to complain, nor to deprecate my way of life. Yet at bottom it has been nothing but work and worry, and I can go so far as to say that in all my seventy-five years I have not truly felt at ease for four weeks on end. . . . My real happiness has been my creative mind and work. . . . A widely known name and high position in life—these are good things. Yet with all my repute and estate I have not got beyond the point of keeping silent when others have their say, lest I give offense.

Now they are saying once again that I am a servant and lackey of princes. As though that meant anything! Is it indeed a tyrant I am serving? A despot? Do I serve one who but indulges his pleasures at the people's expense? Such princes and such times are far behind us, thank God! For half a century I have been most intimately associated with the Grand Duke, and for half a century I have striven and worked with him; but I would have to lie, were I to say I knew a single day when the Grand Duke did not think or do something for the country's welfare, something calculated to improve the lot of the individual. As for him personally, what does his princely estate bring him but work and trouble! Is his home, his dress, his table perchance better than

besser bestellt als die eines wohlhabenden Privatmannes? Man gehe nur in unsere Seestädte und man wird Küche und Keller eines angesehenen Kaufmanns besser bestellt finden als die seinigen.

Ich bin nicht zum tragischen Dichter geboren, weil meine Natur konziliant ist; daher kann der rein tragische Fall mich nicht interessieren, welcher eigentlich von Haus aus unversöhnlich sein muß, und in dieser übrigens so äußerst platten Welt kommt mir das Unversöhnliche ganz absurd vor.

Bei dem vielen Zeug, das ich vorhabe, würde ich verzweifeln, wenn nicht die große Ordnung, in der ich meine Papiere halte, mich in den Stand setzte, zu jeder Stunde überall einzugreifen, jede Stunde in ihrer Art zu nützen und eins nach dem andern vorwärts zu schieben.

Hierbei werd' ich veranlaßt, dir etwas Verwunderliches zu vermelden und zu vertrauen, daß ich nämlich nach einer strengen schnellen Resolution alles Zeitungslesen abgeschafft habe. Seit den sechs Wochen, daß ich die sämtlichen französischen und deutschen Zeitungen unter ihrem Kreuzband liegen lasse, ist es unsäglich, was ich für Zeit gewann, und was ich alles wegschaffe.

those of a well-to-do private person? Just visit one of our port cities, and you will see kitchen and cellar of any respected merchant to be better than the Grand Duke's.

I was not born to be a tragic poet because I am conciliatory by nature. For this reason I cannot be interested in the merely tragic, which by its very nature must be irreconciliable, and in this very shallow world the irreconciliable appears to me quite absurd.

In the face of my many plans and projects I would despair but for the meticulous order in which I keep my papers, which enables me to turn to anything at any time, to take advantage of every hour in its own way, and to carry one thing after the other a step farther.

This gives me occasion to report and confide something odd to you, namely that following a stern and swift resolution I have done away with all newspaper reading. It is unbelievable how much time I have gained and how much I have accomplished in the six weeks since I have let all the French and German newspapers rest in their wrappers.

Man liest viel zuviel geringe Sachen, womit man die Zeit verdirbt, und wovon man nichts weiter hat. Man sollte eigentlich immer nur das lesen, was man bewundert.

Nun glaube ich auf dem rechten Weg zu sein, da ich mich immerfort als einen Reisenden betrachte, der vielem entsagt, um vieles zu genießen.

Kein Segen kommt der Arbeit gleich, und nur der Mensch, welcher sein Leben lang gearbeitet hat, kann sagen: ich habe gelebt.

We read far too much that is trivial, that merely passes the time, without further profit. We ought really to read only what we admire.

Now do I believe to be on the right road, since I persist in regarding myself as a traveler who renounces much in order to enjoy much.

No blessing is equal to the blessings of work. Only life-long work entitles a man to say: I have lived.

Was man auch gegen solche Sammlungen sagen kann, welche die Autoren zerstückelt mitteilen, sie bringen doch manche gute Wirkung hervor. Sind wir doch nicht immer so gut gefaßt und so geistreich, daß wir ein ganzes Werk nach seinem Wert in uns aufzunehmen vermöchten. Streichen wir nicht in einem Buch Stellen an, die sich unmittelbar auf uns beziehen?

Whatever one may say against such collections which present authors in fragments, they do produce some good effects; for we are not always in the mood nor can we always rally our intellectual powers to absorb an entire work on its own merits. Is it not true that we mark passages in books, passages that are of special significance to us?

Aber was gehörte dazu, die Erde nicht allein unter sich liegen zu lassen und sich auf einen höheren Geburtsort zu berufen, sondern auch Niedrigkeit und Armut, Spott, und Verachtung, Schmach und Elend, Leiden und Tod als göttlich anzuerkennen, ja Sünde selbst und Verbrechen nicht als Hindernisse, sondern als Fördernisse des Heiligen zu verehren und liebzugewinnen.

Welchen Weg mußte die Menschheit nicht machen, bis sie dahin gelangte, auch gegen Schuldige gelind, gegen Verbrecher schonend, gegen Unmenschliche menschlich zu sein! . . . Des Schönen sind die Menschen selten fähig, öfter des Guten; und wie hoch müssen wir daher diejenigen halten, die dieses mit großen Aufopferungen zu befördern suchten!

Doch unter allen Entdeckungen und Überzeugungen möchte nichts eine größere Wirkung auf den menschlichen Geist hervorgebracht haben als die Lehre des Kopernikus. Kaum war die Welt als rund anerkannt und in sich selbst abgeschlossen, so sollte sie auf das ungeheure Vorrecht Verzicht tun, der Mittelpunkt des Weltalls zu sein. Vielleicht ist noch nie eine größere Forderung an die Menschheit geschehen; denn was ging nicht alles durch diese Anerkennung in Dunst und Rauch auf: ein zweites Paradies, eine Welt der Unschuld, Dichtkunst und Frömmigkeit, das Zeugnis der Sinne, die Überzeugung eines poetisch-religiösen Glaubens; kein Wunder, daß man dies alles nicht wollte fahren lassen, daß man sich auf alle Weise einer solchen Lehre

What would it not take, not to let the whole world merely lie beneath one, invoking a higher nativity, but rather to acknowledge as divine even lowliness and poverty, scorn and contempt, shame and misery, suffering and death—indeed, to honor and cherish even sin and transgression, not as obstacles, but as aids on the road to sanctity!

How far mankind had to travel before reaching the point of showing mildness to the guilty, mercy to the criminal, humanity to the inhuman! . . . Men are rarely responsive to the beautiful, more often to the good, and we must hold in the highest esteem those who at great sacrifice have sought to foster goodness!

Among all discoveries and postulates perhaps none has exerted a greater effect on the human mind than the Copernican theory. Scarcely was the world acknowledged to be round and complete in itself, when it was asked to renounce the enormous privilege of being the center of the universe. No greater challenge was perhaps ever issued to mankind, for many things went up in smoke with its acceptance— a second paradise, a world of innocence, poetry and piety, the testimony of our senses, the convictions of romantic faith. Small wonder people were reluctant to let all this go, that they opposed by every means

entgegensetzte, die denjenigen, der sie annahm, zu einer bisher unbekannten, ja ungeahnten Denkfreiheit und Großheit der Gesinnung berechtigte und aufforderte.

Schiller erscheint immer im absoluten Besitz seiner erhabenen Natur; er ist so groß am Teetisch, wie er es im Staatsrat gewesen sein würde. Nichts geniert ihn, nichts engt ihn ein, nichts zieht den Flug seiner Gedanken herab; was in ihm von großen Ansichten lebt, geht immer frei heraus, ohne Rücksicht und ohne Bedenken. Das war ein rechter Mensch, und so sollte man auch sein! Wir andere dagegen fühlen uns immer bedingt, die Personen, die Gegenstände, die uns umgeben, haben auf uns ihren Einfluß; der Teelöffel geniert uns, wenn er von Gold ist, da er von Silber sein sollte; und so, durch tausend Rücksichten paralysiert, kommen wir nicht dazu, was etwa Großes in unserer Natur sein möchte, frei herauszulassen. Wir sind die Sklaven der Gegenstände, und erscheinen gering oder bedeutend, je nachdem uns diese zusammenziehen oder zu freier Ausdehnung Raum geben.

Jedes Auftreten von Christus, jede seiner Äußerungen gehen dahin, das Höhere anschaulich zu machen. Immer von dem Gemeinen steigt er hinauf, hebt er hinauf, und weil dies bei Sünden und Gebrechen am auffallendsten ist, kommt dergleichen gar manches vor. . . . Schillern war eben diese echte Christustendenz eingeboren: er berührte nichts Gemeines, ohne es zu veredeln. Seine innere Beschäftigung ging dahin.

a doctrine which challenged and empowered those who embraced it to practice a hitherto unheard-of freedom of thought and greatness of mind.

Schiller always appears in absolute possession of his lofty nature; he is as great at the tea table as he would have been in a privy council. Nothing discommodes him, nothing constrains him, nothing draws down the flight of his thought; whatever great views dwell within him always issue freely, without hesitation or reservation. He was a real man, and that is the way to be! The rest of us always feel circumscribed—the people and objects all about exert their influence on us; we are troubled because the teaspoon is of gold, when it should be of silver; and thus, paralyzed by a thousand and one considerations, we never get to the point of allowing free play to whatever greatness may be burgeoning within us. We are the slaves of things, and we appear trivial or important according as they contract us or give us room for free expansion.

Every appearance of Christ, each of his utterances, is to the end of exemplifying the higher life. Ever does he rise and exalt from the common, and since this is most noteworthy in sin and infirmity, many such instances occur. . . . This true spirit of Christ was innate in Schiller. He never touched anything common without ennobling it. Such was his inner preoccupation.

Seit der Zeit, daß ich Ihnen nicht geschrieben habe, sind mir wenig gute Tage geworden. Ich dachte, mich selbst zu verlieren, und verliere nun den Freund und in demselben die Hälfte meines Daseins. Eigentlich sollte ich eine neue Lebensweise anfangen, aber dazu ist in meinen Jahren auch kein Weg mehr. Ich sehe also jetzt nur jeden Tag unmittelbar vor mich hin und tue das nächste, ohne an eine weitere Folge zu denken.

Und hinter ihm, in wesenlosem Scheine,
Lag, was uns alle bändigt, das Gemeine.

Suchst du das Höchste, das Größte? Die Pflanze kann
    es dich lehren.
Was sie willenlos ist, sei du es wollend—das ist's!

In oberflächlicher Beschauung einer Bibliothek fühlt man sich in der Gegenwart eines großen Kapitals, das geräuschlos unberechenbare Zinsen spendet.

Eigentlich lernen wir nur von Büchern, die wir nicht beurteilen können. Der Autor eines Buches, das wir beurteilen könnten, müßte von uns lernen.

Alles Gescheite ist schon gedacht worden; man muß nur versuchen, es noch einmal zu denken.

Few good days have been vouchsafed me since I last wrote you. I thought to lose myself, only to lose my friend [Schiller] and with him half my life. I ought, indeed, to embark on a new way of life, but at my age no such way is left. All I now see before me is the day that comes up, and I do the next thing, without thought of what will ensue further.

Behind him lay, in waning haze reflected,
The coarse-grained stuff that keeps us all subjected.

If it's the greatest, the highest you seek, the plant
   can direct you.
Strive to become through your will what, without
   will, it is.

On surface contemplation of a library one feels as though in the presence of a vast capital silently yielding incalculable interest.

We really learn only from books we cannot judge. The author of a book we were able to evaluate should learn from us.

All the clever thoughts have long since been thought. What matters is to think them anew.

Man sollte alle Tage wenigstens ein kleines Lied hören, ein gutes Gedicht lesen, ein treffliches Gemälde sehen, und wenn es möglich zu machen wäre, einige vernünftige Worte sprechen.

Die guten Vorsätze im Menschen, die Grundsätze, die immer wieder von der Natur überwältigt werden, sind wie die Reinigung, Scheuerung und Schmückung an Sonn-, Fest-und Ehrentagen. Man wird zwar immer wieder schmutzig, aber es ist doch gut, daß man durch solche partielle Reinigung die Reinlichkeit überhaupt nicht unmöglich macht.

Glückselig der, dessen Welt innerhalb des Hauses ist.

Willst du dich am Ganzen erquicken,
So mußt du das Ganze im Kleinsten erblicken.

Willst du immer weiter schweifen?
Sieh, das Gute liegt so nah.
Lerne nur das Glück ergreifen,
Denn das Glück ist immer da.

Im Atemholen sind zweierlei Gnaden:
Die Luft einziehen, sich ihrer entladen;
Jenes bedrängt, dieses erfrischt;
So wunderbar ist das Leben gemischt.
Du danke Gott, wenn er dich preßt,
Und dank ihm, wenn er dich wieder entläßt.

Every day one should at least hear one little song, read one good poem, see one fine painting and—if at all possible—speak a few sensible words.

Man's good intentions, his resolutions which are ever and again overwhelmed by nature, are like the bathing and scrubbing and dressing-up we do on Sundays and holidays and special occasions. True, we do get dirty again, but at least such partial cleansing serves to prevent cleanliness from being discredited altogether.

Fortunate he whose world lies within the home.

If the entire is to feed thy soul,
Then in the littlest thou must see the whole.

Why forever roam and waver?
Look, the good is always here.
Learn to win the moment's favor.
Lady luck is always near.

In taking breath thou hast two kinds of blessing:
The air intracting, the air egressing.
The one feels anxious, the other refreshed.
Thus strangely too is thy life enmeshed.
Thou thank thy God Which presses thee;
And thank him further when He sets thee free.

Unglück ist auch gut. Ich habe viel in der Krankheit gelernt, das ich nirgends in meinem Leben hätte lernen können.

Jedes Bedürfnis, dessen wirkliche Befriedigung versagt ist, nötigt zum Glauben.

Die Gottheit ist im Werdenden und sich Verwandelnden, aber nicht im Gewordenen und Erstarrten.

Man geht nie weiter, als wenn man nicht mehr weiß, wohin man geht.

Je älter ich werde, je mehr vertrau ich auf das Gesetz, wonach die Ros' und die Lilie blüht.

Der Zweck des Lebens ist das Leben selbst.

Durch ein paar Züge aus dem Becher der wahren Liebe hält die Natur für ein Leben voll Mühe schadlos.

Der Umgang mit Frauen ist das Element guter Sitten.

Man erziehe die Knaben zu Dienern und die Mädchen zu Müttern, so wird es überall wohl stehen.

Misery too has its virtues. I have learned much in illness that I could have learned nowhere else in my life.

Every need denied real gratification constrains to faith.

Divinity inheres in growth and change, not in frozen finality.

One never goes farther than when one no longer knows whither one goes.

The older I grow, the more I trust in the law by which the rose and the lily bloom.

Life's purpose is life itself.

Nature, with a few drafts from the cup of true love, repays us for a lifetime of stress and strain.

Converse with women is the school of good manners.

One should train boys to serve and girls to be mothers; all will then be well everywhere.

Friedrich Schiller
Drawing by Francis Reisz
after a sculpture by J. H. Dannecker

Betrachten wir uns in jeder Lage des Lebens, so finden wir, daß wir äußerlich bedingt sind, vom ersten Atemzug bis zum letzten; daß uns aber jedoch die höchste Freiheit übrig geblieben ist, uns innerhalb unsrer selbst dergestalt auszubilden, daß wir uns mit der sittlichen Weltordnung in Einklang setzen und, was auch für Hindernisse sich hervortun, dadurch mit uns selbst zum Frieden gelangen können.—Dies ist bald gesagt und geschrieben, steht aber auch nur als Aufgabe vor uns, deren Auflösung wir unsre Tage durchaus zu widmen haben. Jeder Morgen ruft zu: das Gehörige zu tun und das Mögliche zu erwarten.

When we regard ourselves in the many situations life brings, we find that from first breath to last we are conditioned by external factors. Yet is that highest freedom left to us—to perfect ourselves within, so that we shall come into harmony with the moral world order and attain peace with ourselves, no matter what obstacles may emerge.— This is easily said and written, yet it is no more than a goal before us, to the achievement of which we must thoroughly dedicate ourselves. Every day challenges us to do what is to be done and to expect whatever is possible.

Niemand ist mehr Sklave, als der sich für frei hält, ohne es zu sein.

Alles, was unsern Geist befreit, ohne uns die Herrschaft über uns selbst zu geben, ist verderblich.

Wer mit dem Leben spielt,
Kommt nie zurecht;
Wer sich nicht selbst befiehlt,
Bleibt immer ein Knecht.

Es darf sich einer nur für frei erklären, so fühlt er sich den Augenblick als bedingt. Wagt er es, sich für bedingt zu erklären, so fühlt er sich frei.

Unser Leben ist, wie das Ganze in dem wir enthalten sind, auf eine unbegreifliche Weise aus Freiheit und Notwendigkeit zusammengesetzt. Unser Wollen ist ein Vorausverkünden dessen, was wir unter allen Umständen tun werden. Diese Umstände aber ergreifen uns auf ihre eigene Weise. Das Was liegt in uns, das Wie hängt selten von uns ab, nach dem Warum dürfen wir nicht fragen. . . .

Des Menschen größtes Verdienst bleibt wohl, wenn er die Umstände so viel als möglich bestimmt, und sich so wenig als möglich von ihnen bestimmen läßt.

So gewiß ist der allein glücklich und groß, der weder zu herrschen noch zu gehorchen hat, um etwas zu sein.

The most enslaved is he who thinks himself free without being free.

Anything that liberates our spirit without giving us mastery over ourselves is pernicious.

Who lives by sleight of hand
Is bound to fall.
Who fails in self-command
Remains a thrall.

Let a man but declare himself free, he will instantly feel limited. But let him be bold enough to declare himself limited, and he will feel a sense of freedom.

Like the whole in which we are contained, our life is incomprehensibly composed of freedom and necessity. Our willing is a harbinger of what we shall do in all circumstances. These circumstances, however, seize upon us in their own way. The What lies within us, the How seldom depends on ourselves, nor must we inquire after the Why. . . .

Perhaps the greatest thing that can be said to a man's credit is that he gains the greatest possible control over circumstances, that he lets circumstances have the least possible control over him.

Assuredly he alone is happy and possessed of greatness who, to be something, needs neither to rule nor to obey.

Die Menschen werfen sich im Politischen wie auf dem Krankenlager von einer Seite zur andern, in der Meinung, besser zu liegen.

Wie man denn niemals mehr von Freiheit reden hört, als wenn eine Partei die andere unterjochen will und es auf weiter nichts abgesehen ist, als daß Gewalt, Einfluß und Vermögen aus einer Hand in die andere gehen. Freiheit ist die leise Parole heimlich Verschworener, das laute Feldgeschrei der öffentlich Umwälzenden, ja das Losungswort der Despotie selbst, wenn sie ihre unterjochte Masse gegen den Feind vorführt und ihr von auswärtigem Druck Erlösung auf alle Zeiten verspricht.

Gesetzgeber und Revolutionäre, die Gleichheit und Freiheit zugleich verspechen, sind Phantasten und Charlatans.

Sie streiten sich, so heißt's, um Freiheitsrechte.
Genau besehn, sind's Knechte gegen Knechte.

Freiheit ist nichts als die Möglichkeit, unter allen Bedingungen das Vernünftige zu tun.

Welche Regierung die beste sei? Diejenige, die uns lehrt, uns selbst zu regieren.

In politics as on a sickbed men toss from side to side in hope of lying more comfortably.

Never do we hear more talk of freedom than when one party wants to subjugate the other, with nothing else the issue than that power, influence, and property pass from one hand to another. Freedom is the whispered password of stealthy conspirators, the clamorous battle cry of avowed revolutionaries, indeed, the slogan of despotism itself, as it leads its subjugated masses forward against the foe promising surcease from oppression for all time.

Legislators and revolutionaries who promise both equality and liberty are visionaries and charlatans.

They fight, we hear, to safeguard human rights.
Look close and see it's slave 'gainst slave that fights.

Freedom is nothing more than the opportunity to do what is reasonable in all circumstances.

Which government is the best? That which teaches us to govern ourselves.

Freiwillige Abhängigkeit ist der schönste Zu-
stand, und wie wäre der möglich ohne Liebe?

Voluntary dependence is the fairest state of all—and but for love, how would it be possible?

Die ersten Liebesneigungen einer unverdorbenen Jugend nehmen durchaus eine geistige Wendung. Die Natur scheint zu wollen, daß ein Geschlecht in dem andern das Gute und Schöne sinnlich gewahr werde.

Gegen große Vorzüge eines andern gibt es kein Rettungsmittel als die Liebe.

So eine wahre, warme Freude ist nicht in der Welt, als eine große Seele zu sehen, die sich gegen einen öffnet.

Der liebt nicht, der die Fehler des Geliebten nicht für Tugenden hält.

Die wenigsten Menschen lieben an dem andern das, was er ist, nur das, was sie ihm leihen; sich, ihre Vorstellung von ihm, lieben sie.

Freudvoll
Und leidvoll,
Gedankenvoll sein,
Langen
Und bangen
In schwebender Pein,
Himmelhoch jauchzend,
Zum Tode betrübt—
Glücklich allein
Ist die Seele, die liebt.

The first amorous inclinations of an unspoiled youth commonly take a spiritual turn. Nature seems to desire one sex to become sensually aware of the good and beautiful in the other.

Confronted with great merits, there is no resistance but love.

There is no joy in the world so true and warm as to witness a great soul opening toward one.

He loves not who does not see the faults of the beloved as virtues.

Few people love others for what they are. Rather do they love them for what they project into them. What they really love is themselves, their idea of the other.

Gladdened
And saddened
In thoughtful refrain,
Worried
And sorried
In lingering pain,
Cheered to high heaven,
Depressed to deep gloom,
Happy is fain
But a soul in love's bloom.

Eine Liebe kann wohl im Nu entstehen, und jede echte Neigung muß irgend einmal gleich dem Blitze plötzlich aufgeflammt sein; aber wer wird sich denn gleich heiraten, wenn man liebt? Liebe ist etwas Ideelles, Heiraten etwas Reelles, und nie verwechselt man ungestraft das Ideelle mit dem Reellen. Solch ein wichtiger Lebensschritt will allseitig überlegt sein und längere Zeit hindurch, ob auch alle individuellen Beziehungen, wenigstens die meisten, zusammenpassen.

Wer mir den Ehestand angreift, wer mir durch Wort, ja durch Tat, diesen Grund aller sittlichen Gesellschaft untergräbt, der hat es mit mir zu tun! . . . Die Ehe ist der Anfang und der Gipfel aller Kultur. Sie macht den Rohen mild, und der Gebildete hat keine bessere Gelegenheit, seine Milde zu beweisen. Unauflöslich muß sie sein; denn sie bringt so vieles Glück, daß alles einzelne Unglück dagegen gar nicht zu rechnen ist. Und was will man von Unglück reden? Ungeduld ist es, die den Menschen von Zeit zu Zeit anfällt, und dann beliebt er, sich unglücklich zu finden. Lasse man den Augenblick vorübergehen und man wird sich glücklich preisen, daß ein so lange Bestandenes noch besteht. Sich zu trennen gibt's gar keinen hinlänglichen Grund. Der menschliche Zustand ist so hoch in Leiden und Freuden gesetzt, daß gar nicht berechnet werden kann, was ein Paar Gatten einander schuldig werden. Es ist eine unendliche Schuld, die nur durch die Ewigkeit abgetragen werden kann. Unbequem mag es manchmal sein, das glaub ich wohl und das ist eben recht.

Love may indeed arise in a trice, and at some time all true affection must have flared up suddenly, like a flash of lightning; but who will want to go off and marry instantly, just for love? Love is something ideal, while matrimony is real, and the one is never with impunity confounded with the other. So important a step in life wants careful consideration, over a longer period of time, to establish whether all—or at least most—of the qualities of the partners are compatible.

Whoever attacks the institution of matrimony, whoever undermines this foundation-stone of all civilized society in word, let alone deed, will have me to reckon with! . . . Marriage is the beginning and the pinnacle of all culture. It tempers the uncouth while affording the educated his finest opportunity for demonstrating good nature. It must be indissoluble; for it brings so much happiness that all individual unhappiness is as nothing against it. And why speak of unhappiness? It is impatience that assails man from time to time, and then he chooses to think himself unhappy. Let the moment pass and he will praise his good fortune that something so well established still endures. There is no adequate reason whatever to separate. The human condition rates so high in sorrow and joy that the debt spouses owe each other is incalculable. So infinite is it that only eternity can extinguish it. Irksome it may be at times, I can well believe, and that is good and proper. We are, after

Sind wir nicht auch mit dem Gewissen verheiratet, das wir oft gerne los sein möchten, weil es unbequemer ist, als uns je ein Mann oder eine Frau werden könnte.

Was liegt daran, ob einige Paare sich prügeln und das Leben verbittern, wenn nur der allgemeine Begriff der Heiligkeit der Ehe aufrecht bleibt.

Im Ehestand muß man sich manchmal streiten, denn dadurch erfährt man was von einander.

Ein wenig Geiz schadet dem Weibe nichts, so übel sie die Verschwendung kleidet. Freigebigkeit ist eine Tugend, die dem Manne ziemt, und Festhalten ist die Tugend eines Weibes. So hat es die Natur gewollt, und unser Urteil wird im ganzen immer naturgemäß ausfallen.

Wenn ein kluger Mann der Frau befiehlt,
Dann sei es um ein Großes gespielt;
Will die Frau dem Mann befehlen,
So muß sie das Große im Kleinen wählen.

Eine stille ernsthafte Frau ist übel daran mit einem lustigen Manne. Ein ernsthafter Mann nicht so mit einer lustigen Frau.

Welche Frau hat einen guten Mann,
Der sieht man's am Gesicht wohl an.

Vermag die Liebe alles zu dulden, so vermag sie noch viel mehr, alles zu ersetzen.

all, also wedded to our conscience, of which we oft would be rid, for it is more irksome than husband or wife could ever be.

What matter if a few couples trade blows and make life miserable for each other, if but the general concept of the sanctity of marriage be maintained.

Quarrels between married people are necessary at times, for in this way they learn something about each other.

A touch of avarice does no harm in a woman, whom wastefulness ill befits. Generosity is a virtue that becomes the man, while a tight hand is woman's virtue. Thus has nature ordained, and by and large our judgment will always comport with nature.

When a shrewd man his wife command,
Let major issues be at hand;
But would a wife command her spouse,
The big within the little she must choose.

A quiet, serious-minded wife is ill off with a light-hearted husband. Not so a grave man with a merry woman.

By a wife's face it may be known
That a good husband she doth own.

If love can put up with everything, it can do still more: take the place of all else.

Die wahre Poesie kündigt sich dadurch an, daß sie, als ein weltliches Evangelium, durch innere Heiterkeit, durch äußeres Behagen, uns von den irdischen Lasten zu befreien weiß, die auf uns drücken. Wie ein Luftballon hebt sie uns mit dem Ballast, der uns anhängt, in höhere Regionen und läßt die verwirrten Irrgänge der Erde in Vogelperspektive vor uns entwickelt daliegen. Die muntersten wie die ernstesten Werke haben den gleichen Zweck, durch eine glückliche, geistreiche Darstellung so Lust als Schmerz zu mäßigen.

True poetry identifies itself as a secular gospel, marked by inward serenity and outward pleasure, serving to lift the earthly burdens that oppress us. Like a balloon it makes us soar, with all the ballast that clings to us, up into higher regions, unrolling earth's confusing mazes in bird's-eye view before us. Light-hearted or grave in tone, poetry pursues the same purpose: to moderate both pleasure and pain by spirited and felicitous portrayal.

Es ist ein großer Unterschied, ob der Dichter zum Allgemeinen das Besondere sucht oder im Besonderen das Allgemeine schaut. Aus jener Art entsteht Allegorie, wo das Besondere nur als Beispiel, als Exempel des Allgemeinen gilt; die letztere aber ist eigentlich die Natur der Poesie, sie spricht ein Besonderes aus, ohne ans Allgemeine zu denken oder darauf hinzuweisen. Wer nun dieses Besondere lebendig faßt, erhält zugleich das Allgemeine mit, ohne es gewahr zu werden, oder erst spät.

Solange der Dichter bloß seine wenigen, subjektiven Empfindungen ausspricht, ist er noch keiner zu nennen; aber sobald er die Welt sich anzueignen und auszusprechen weiß, ist er ein Poet. Und dann ist er unerschöpflich und kann immer neu sein, wogegen aber eine subjektive Natur ihr bißchen Inneres bald ausgesprochen hat und zuletzt in Manier zu Grunde geht.

Der echte, gesetzgebende Künstler strebt nach Kunstwahrheit, der gesetzlose, der einem blinden Trieb folgt, nach Naturwirklichkeit; durch jenen wird die Kunst zum höchsten Gipfel, durch diesen auf die niedrigste Stufe gebracht.

Es ist immer ein Zeichen einer unproduktiven Zeit, wenn sie so ins Kleinliche und Technische geht, und ebenso ist es ein Zeichen eines unproduktiven Individuums, wenn es sich mit dergleichen befaßt.

It makes a great difference whether the poet seeks the special in the general or whether he views the general within the special. The former gives rise to allegory, where the special serves only as the example, the specific case of the general, while the latter is essentially of the nature of poetry, giving voice to the special, without thought or hint of the general. Whoever captures the special in the flesh, gets the general along with it, without growing aware of it, or growing aware of it only late.

A poet who merely utters his own few subjective sentiments scarcely deserves the name; but as soon as he is able to make the world his own and lend it voice, he becomes a poet; and then he is inexhaustible and can be unendingly new. A subjective nature soon exhausts its sparse content and destroys itself in mannerism.

The true, law-making artist strives for the truth of art, the lawless, following but blind instinct, for the realism of nature. The one brings art to its highest pinnacle, the other to its lowest ebb.

An age that is petty and overtechnical bespeaks its barrenness; and similar preoccupations in an individual are equally a sign of unproductivity.

Einbildungskraft wird durch die Kunst, besonders durch Poesie geregelt. Es ist nichts fürchterlicher als Einbildungskraft ohne Geschmack.

Es beschränkt sich selten ein Künstler auf das, was er vermag, die meisten wollen mehr tun, als sie können und gehen gar zu gern über den Kreis hinaus, den die Natur ihrem Talent gesetzt hat.

Das ist aber eben das Wesen der Dilettanten, daß sie die Schwierigkeiten nicht kennen, die in einer Sache liegen, und daß sie immer etwas unternehmen vollen, wozu sie keine Kräfte haben.

Dilettanten und besonders Frauen haben von der Poesie sehr schwache Begriffe. Sie glauben gewöhnlich, wenn sie nur das Technische los hätten, so hätten sie das Wesen und wären gemachte Leute; allein sie sind sehr in der Irre.

Um Prosa zu schreiben, muß man etwas zu sagen haben; wer aber nichts zu sagen hat, der kann doch Verse und Reime machen, wo denn ein Wort das andere gibt und zuletzt etwas herauskommt, das zwar nichts ist, aber doch aussieht, als wäre es etwas.

Die Dunkelheit gewisser Maximen ist nur relativ: nicht alles ist dem Hörenden deutlich zu machen, was dem Ausübenden einleuchtet.

Imagination is kept within bounds by art, especially by poetry. There is nothing worse than imagination without taste.

Artists seldom limit themselves to what lies within their capacity. Most of them want to do more than they are able and want to go beyond the limitations nature has set their talents.

That is precisely the nature of the amateur—he does not know the difficulties inherent in a given task and is ever bent on undertaking one for which he has no equipment.

Amateurs, and especially women, have but a feeble comprehension of poetry. They commonly believe if they but knew the techniques they had grasped the whole of it and were on Easy Street. How very much mistaken they are!

To write prose, one must have something to say. Those who have nothing to say may still fashion verses and rhymes, one word giving rise to the next, with something resulting that is actually nothing, but looks as though it were something.

The obscurity of certain maxims is but relative. Not everything that is obvious to the formulator can be made clear to the listener.

Wer einem Autor Dunkelheit vorwerfen will, sollte erst sein eigenes Inneres beschauen, ob es denn da auch recht hell ist: in der Dämmerung wird eine sehr deutliche Schrift unlesbar.

Wer bei seinen Arbeiten nicht schon ganz seinen Lohn dahin hat, ehe das Werk öffentlich erscheint, der ist übel daran.

Die Manier will immer fertig sein und hat keinen Genuß an der Arbeit. Das echte, wahrhaft große Talent aber findet sein höchstes Glück in der Ausführung.

Die Poeten schreiben alle, als wären sie krank und die ganze Welt ein Lazarett! Alle sprechen sie von den Leiden und dem Jammer der Erde, und von den Freuden des Jenseits, und unzufrieden wie schon alle sind, hetzt einer den andern in noch größere Unzufriedenheit hinein. Das ist ein wahrer Mißbrauch der Poesie, die uns doch eigentlich dazu gegeben ist, um die kleinen Zwiste des Lebens auszugleichen, und den Menschen mit der Welt und seinem Zustande zufrieden zu machen. Aber die jetzige Generation fürchtet sich vor aller echten Kraft, und nur bei der Schwäche ist es ihr gemütlich und poetisch zu Sinne.

Nach meiner Überzeugung soll die Kunst, wenn sie sich mit dem Schmerz verbindet, denselben nur aufregen, um ihn zu mildern und in höhere, tröstliche Gefühle aufzulösen; und ich werde in diesem Sinne

Those who reproach an author for being obscure should first look inside themselves, to see how much light there is in there. At dusk a plain hand becomes illegible.

Whoever fails to find his full reward before his work is published—in the work itself—is to be pitied.

Hacks always want to get done with it, finding no pleasure in the work itself. A truly great talent finds its highest joy in the execution.

The poets all write as though they were sick and the whole world a hospital. They speak of the grief and sorrow of this world and of the joys of the hereafter; and discontented as they are, one and all, each incites the other to ever greater dissatisfaction. This is indeed misusing poetry, which is really meant to smooth over life's petty strife and make man content with the world and his own state. But the present generation fears all genuine strength and feels at ease and in a poetic mood only in the face of weakness.

Art, when associated with pain, should in my conviction arouse it but to ameliorate and dissolve it into higher, more comforting sentiments; and in this

weniger das, was wir verloren haben, als das, was uns übrig bleibt, darzustellen suchen.

Alle Poesie soll belehrend sein, aber unmerklich; sie soll den Menschen aufmerksam machen, wovon sich zu belehren wert wäre; er muß die Lehre selbst daraus ziehen wie aus dem Leben.

Ein gutes Kunstwerk kann und wird zwar moralische Folgen haben, aber moralische Zwecke vom Künstler fordern, heißt ihm sein Handwerk verderben.

Die Musik aber, so wenig als irgend eine Kunst, vermag auf Moralität zu wirken, und immer ist es falsch, wenn man solche Leistungen von ihnen verlangt. Philosophie und Religion vermögen es allein; Pietät und Pflicht müssen aufgeregt werden, und solche Erweckungen werden die Künste nur zufällig veranlassen. Was sie aber vermögen und wirken, das ist eine Milderung roher Sitten.

Eine Erscheinung wie Mozart bleibt immer ein Wunder, das nicht weiter zu erklären ist. Doch wie wollte die Gottheit überall Wunder zu tun Gelegenheit finden, wenn sie es nicht zuweilen in außerordentlichen Individuen versuchte, die wir anstaunen und nicht begreifen, woher sie kommen.

Das ist eben recht, daß man nicht fort kann und gezwungen ist, auch das Schlechte zu hören und sehen. Da wird man recht vom Haß gegen das Schlechte durchdrungen und kommt dadurch zu einer besseren Einsicht des Guten.

sense I shall seek to represent less what we have lost than what is left to us.

All poetry should be instructive, though imperceptibly so. It should draw man's attention to what is worth learning about. The lesson itself he must draw as from life.

A fine work of art may and will have moral effects, but to demand moral aims of the artist is to ruin his craft.

Music has no effect on morals, any more than any other art, and to expect this of any of the arts is futile. Only philosophy and religion have this power to stimulate devotion and a sense of duty. If the arts do arouse these virtues, it is purely by chance. What they can do is to soften uncouthness.

A phenomenon like Mozart always remains a mystery, not susceptible to further explanation; yet indeed, why should God find occasion to work miracles all about and not at times try his hand at extraordinary individuals who astound us and whose provenance we cannot grasp!

It is only right that one cannot sneak away but is compelled to hear and see the bad with the good. This is precisely what fills one with loathing of the bad, providing deeper appreciation of the good.

Den Geschmack kann man nicht am Mittelgut bilden, sondern nur am Allervorzüglichsten.

Der Kopf faßt kein Kunstprodukt, als nur in Gesellschaft mit dem Herzen.

Die originalsten Autoren der neuesten Zeit sind es nicht deswegen, weil sie etwas Neues hervorbringen, sondern allein weil sie fähig sind, dergleichen Dinge zu sagen, als wenn sie vorher niemals wären gesagt gewesen.

Im ganzen ist der Stil eines Schriftstellers ein treuer Abdruck seines Inneren: will jemand einen klaren Stil schreiben, so sei es ihm zuvor klar in seiner Seele; und will jemand einen großartigen Stil schreiben, so habe er einen großartigen Charakter.

Jenes ungestörte, unschuldige, nachtwandlerische Schaffen, wodurch allein etwas Großes gedeihen kann, ist gar nicht mehr möglich. Unsere jetzigen Talente liegen alle auf dem Präsentierteller der Öffentlichkeit. Die täglich an fünfzig verschiedenen Orten erscheinenden kritischen Blätter und der dadurch im Publikum bewirkte Klatsch lassen nichts Gesundes aufkommen. Wer sich heutzutage nicht ganz davon zurückhält und sich nicht mit Gewalt isoliert, ist verloren. Es kommt zwar durch das schlechte, größtenteils negative, ästhetisierende und kritisierende Zeitungswesen eine Art Halbkultur in die Massen, allein dem hervorbringenden Talent ist es ein böses Übel, ein fallendes Gift, das den Baum

Good taste cannot be cultivated with middling things but only with the very best.

The mind can comprehend a work of art only in concert with the heart.

The most original authors of our time are original not because they create anything new but solely because they are able to say the things they say as though none had ever said them before.

All in all, a writer's style is a true reflection of his inward life. Anyone who seeks to write a clear style, let him first achieve clarity of mind; and anyone who seeks to write in the grand manner, let him first achieve grandeur of character.

That undisturbed, innocent, sleepwalking kind of creation, by which alone anything great can flourish, is no longer possible. Our present-day talents all lie open to public view. The critical journals, appearing daily in fifty different places, together with the gossip they engender among the public, permit nothing sound to rise. Unless man today withdraw altogether from such things and isolate himself with the utmost austerity, he is lost. True, the cheap newspapers with their largely negative criticism and pseudo esthetics do propagate a kind of half-culture among the masses, but to the creative talent this is a profound evil, a poison that lays him low, that saps the tree of his creative powers, from the green adorn-

seiner Schöpfungskraft zerstört, vom grünen Schmuck der Blätter bis in das tiefste Mark und in die verborgenste Faser.—Und dann, wie zahm und schwach ist seit den lumpigen paar hundert Jahren nicht das Leben selber geworden! Wo kommt uns noch eine originelle Natur unverhüllt entgegen? Und wo hat einer die Kraft, wahr zu sein und sich zu zeigen?

Könnten Geist und höhere Bildung ein Gemeingut werden, so hätte der Dichter ein gutes Spiel; er könnte immer durchaus wahr sein und brauchte sich nicht zu scheuen, das Beste zu sagen. So aber muß er sich immer in einem gewissen Niveau halten; er hat zu bedenken, daß seine Werke in die Hände einer gemischten Welt kommen, und er hat daher Ursache, sich in acht zu nehmen, daß er der Mehrzahl guter Menschen durch eine zu große Offenheit kein Ärgernis gebe. Und dann ist die Zeit ein wunderlich Ding. Sie ist ein Tyrann, der seine Launen hat und der zu dem, was einer sagt und tut, in jedem Jahrhundert ein ander Gesicht macht. Was den alten Griechen zu sagen erlaubt war, will uns zu sagen nicht mehr anstehen, und was Shakespeares kräftigen Mitmenschen durchaus anmutete, kann der Engländer von heute nicht mehr ertragen, so daß in der neuesten Zeit ein 'Family-Shakespeare' ein gefühltes Bedürfnis wird.

Der Mensch erfährt und genießt nichts, ohne sogleich produktiv zu werden. Dies ist die innerste Eigenschaft der menschlichen Natur. Ja, man darf

ment of its foliage to its innermost marrow and fiber. Then too, how tame and feeble has life itself grown in those wretched few hundred years! Where can we still meet a truly original personality unadorned? And where is there anyone with the power of being truthful and of revealing himself?

If spirit and higher education were the heritage of all, things would be easy for the poet. He could always stick to the truth and need never hesitate to say his best. As it is, he must always keep to a certain level. He must consider that his works will come into the hands of a mixed world, hence has reason to take care lest too much frankness give offense to the majority of good people. Then too, time itself is a curious thing. It is a tyrant with moods of its own. In every century it shows a different face to what people say and do. What was permitted to the ancient Greeks to say is no longer appropriate for us to say, and what Shakespeare's earthy fellow citizens accepted without flinching, the Briton can today no longer tolerate, so that a "family Shakespeare" has become a definitely felt need in our time.

Man learns and enjoys nothing, except he become at once productive. This is the inmost quality of human

ohne Übertreibung sagen, es sei die menschliche Natur selbst.

Jede Produktivität höchster Art, jedes bedeutende Aperçu, jede Erfindung, jeder große Gedanke, der Früchte bringt, steht in niemandes Gewalt und ist über aller irdischer Macht erhaben. Dergleichen hat der Mensch als unverhoffte Geschenke von oben, als reine Kinder Gottes zu betrachten, die er mit freudigem Dank zu empfangen and zu verehren hat. Es ist dem Dämonischen verwandt, das übermächtig mit ihm tut, wie es beliebt, und dem er sich bewußtlos hingibt, während er glaubt, er handle aus eigenem Antriebe. In solchen Fällen ist der Mensch oftmals als Werkzeug einer höheren Weltregierung zu betrachten, als ein würdig befundenes Gefäß zur Aufnahme eines göttlichen Einflusses.

nature. Indeed, one may say without exaggeration it is human nature itself.

All productivity of the highest kind, every significant *aperçu*, every invention, every great thought that bears fruit is beyond man's power, indeed, beyond all earthly power. These things man must regard as surprise gifts from on high, as pure children of God, to be received and honored with joyful gratitude. They are akin to those all-powerful demoniac forces that do with him as they please, to which he unknowingly yields, even as he believes he is acting on his own. In such cases man must often be looked on as the instrument of a higher world order, a vessel found worthy to receive the divine impulse.

Man studiere nicht die Mitgeborenen und Mitstrebenden, sondern große Menschen der Vorzeit, deren Werke seit Jahrhunderten gleichen Wert und gleiches Ansehen behalten haben. Ein wirklich hochbegabter Mensch wird das Bedürfnis dazu ohnehin in sich fühlen, und gerade dieses Bedürfnis des Umgangs mit großen Vorgängern ist das Zeichen einer höheren Anlage. Man studiere Molière, man studiere Shakespeare, aber vor allen Dingen die alten Griechen, und immer die Griechen.

Never mind studying contemporaries and those who strive with you. Study the great men of the past, whose works have maintained their value and stature for centuries. A truly gifted man will naturally so incline; and the desire to delve into the great precursors is the very mark of a higher endowment. Study Molière, study Shakespeare, but above all study the ancient Greeks, ever and always the Greeks.

Jemand sagte: "Was bemüht ihr euch um den Homer? Ihr versteht ihn doch nicht." Darauf antwortet' ich: Versteh ich doch auch Sonne, Mond und Sterne nicht; aber sie gehen über meinem Haupte hin, und ich erkenne mich in ihnen, indem ich sie sehe und ihren regelmäßigen, wunderbaren Gang betrachte, und denke dabei, ob auch wohl etwas aus mir werden könnte.

Der für dichterische und bildnerische Schöpfungen empfängliche Geist fühlt sich dem Altertum gegenüber in den anmutigst-ideellen Naturzustand versetzt, und noch auf den heutigen Tag haben die Homerischen Gesänge die Kraft, uns wenigstens für Augenblicke von der furchtbaren Last zu befreien, welche die Überlieferung von mehreren tausend Jahren auf uns gewälzt hat.

Man denke sich das Große der Alten, vorzüglich der sokratischen Schule, daß sie Quelle und Richtschnur alles Lebens und Tuns vor Augen stellt, nicht zu leerer Spekulation, sondern zu Leben und Tat auffordert. Wenn nun unser Schulunterricht immer auf das Altertum hinweist, das Studium der griechischen und lateinischen Sprache fördert, so können wir uns Glück wünschen, daß diese zu einer höheren Kultur so nötigen Studien niemals rückgängig werden. Denn wenn wir uns dem Altertum gegenüberstellen und es ernstlich in der Absicht anschauen, uns daran zu bilden, so gewinnen wir die Empfindung, als ob wir erst eigentlich zu Menschen würden.

Someone said: "Why trouble yourself about Homer? You will not really understand him." Whereupon I replied: Nor do I understand sun, moon and stars; but they pass overhead, and in seeing them and their marvelously ordered orbits I see myself and think that perhaps something may yet become of me.

Any mind susceptible to creative art or literature feels itself translated into an ideal state of nature and grace when confronting antiquity. To this day the chants of Homer have the power to free us, at least momentarily, from the fearful burden several thousand years of tradition have placed on our shoulders.

One must think of the greatness of the ancients, preeminently the Socratic school, as lying in their putting before our eyes sources and directives for all life and action—not for vain speculation, but as a challenge to living and acting; and if instruction in our schools keeps harking back to antiquity, fosters the study of Greek and Latin, we can but hope fervently that these studies, so essential to higher culture, will never be abolished; for when we confront antiquity, regard it with the purpose of educating ourselves by it, we come to feel that only then do we become men.

Ich für meine Person bin in dem Falle, daß mich das Anschauen des Altertume in jedem seiner Reste in den Zustand versetzt, worin ich fühle, ein Mensch zu sein.

Unter allen Völkerschaften haben die Griechen den Traum des Lebens am schönsten geträumt.

Möge das Studium der griechischen und römischen Literatur immerfort die Basis der höhern Bildung bleiben!

Bisher glaubte die Welt an den Heldensinn einer Lucretia, eines Mucius Scaevola, und ließ sich dadurch erwärmen und begeistern. Jetzt aber kommt die historische Kritik und sagt, daß jene Personen nie gelebt haben, sondern als Fiktionen und Fabeln anzusehen sind, die der große Sinn der Römer erdichtete. Was sollen wir aber mit einer so ärmlichen Wahrheit? Und wenn die Römer groß genug waren, so etwas zu erdichten, so sollen wir wenigstens groß genug sein, daran zu glauben.

Das Altertum setzen wir gern über uns, aber die Nachwelt nicht. Nur ein Vater neidet seinem Sohn nicht das Talent.

Chinesische, indische, ägyptische Altertümer sind immer nur Kuriositäten; es ist sehr wohlgetan, sich und die Welt damit bekannt zu machen; zu sittlicher und ästhetischer Bildung aber werden sie uns wenig fruchten.

As for myself, gazing at antiquity in any of its remnants puts me in a state of feeling myself a man.

Among all the peoples, the Greeks have dreamed the dream of life most beautifully.

May the study of Greek and Roman literature ever remain the basis of higher education!

The world has hitherto believed in the heroism of a Lucretia, or a Mucius Scaevola, and has let itself be fired and inspired by them. Now comes historical criticism and tells us such persons never lived but must be looked on as mere fiction and fable, created by the great spirit of the Romans. What are we to do with so wretched a truth? If the Romans were great enough to create such legends, we should be at least great enough to believe in them.

We are quite willing to acknowledge that the past was better than ourselves, but not that the future will be. Only fathers do not envy their sons' talent.

Chinese, Hindu and Egyptian antiquities always remain curiosities. It is all very well to get to know them and to make them known; but they contribute little to our moral and esthetic education.

Im Grunde aber sind wir alle kollektive Wesen, wir mögen uns stellen, wie wir wollen. Denn wie Weniges haben und sind wir, das wir im reinsten Sinne unser Eigentum nennen! Wir müssen alle empfangen und lernen, sowohl von denen, die vor uns waren, als von denen, die mit uns sind. Selbst das größte Genie würde nicht weit kommen, wenn es alles seinem Innern verdanken wollte. . . . Es ist im Grunde auch alles Torheit, ob einer etwas aus sich habe, oder ob er es von andern habe; . . . die Hauptsache ist, daß man ein großes Wollen habe und Geschick und Beharrlichkeit besitze, es auszuführen.

Wir bringen wohl Fähigkeiten mit, aber unsre Entwicklung verdanken wir tausend Einwirkungen einer großen Welt, aus der wir uns aneignen, was wir können. . . . Ich verdanke den Griechen und Franzosen viel, ich bin Shakespeare, Sterne und Goldsmith Unendliches schuldig geworden. Allein damit sind die Quellen meiner Kultur nicht nachgewiesen, es würde ins Grenzenlose gehen und wäre auch nicht nötig. Die Hauptsache ist, daß man eine Seele habe, die das Wahre liebt und die es aufnimmt, wo sie es findet.

Heinrich der Vierte von Shakespeare: wenn alles verloren wäre, was je, dieserart geschrieben, zu uns gekommen, so könnte man Poesie und Rhetorik daraus vollkommen wiederherstellen.

At bottom we are all collective creatures, whatever we may say. How little we have and we are that we may in the purest sense call our own! All of us must receive and learn, from those who have gone before us as well as from those who are with us. Even the greatest genius would not get very far, if he tried to rely on his own resources alone. . . . Then too, it is at bottom folly to trouble whether one owes everything to oneself or is indebted to others; . . . the main thing is to be strong in will power and to be possessed of the skill and pertinacity to carry out one's will.

True, we are born with certain innate capacities, but we owe our development to a thousand and one influences from the great world, from which we appropriate what we may. . . . I owe much to the Greeks and the French, and I have become indebted beyond telling to Shakespeare, Sterne and Goldsmith. Yet they all do not exhaust the sources of my culture—to do so would transcend all limits and would also be quite pointless. The main thing is that one have a soul which loves truth and welcomes it wherever it is found.

King Henry the Fourth by Shakespeare: If everything that has been handed down to us of such writings were lost, poetry and rhetoric could be perfectly reconstructed from it.

Zu den glücklichen Umständen, welche Shakespeares gebornes großes Talent frei und rein entwickelten, gehört auch, daß er Protestant war; er hätte sonst wie Kalidasa und Calderon Absurditäten verherrlichen müssen.

Nur einen Begriff zu haben, daß so etwas von Kunst in der Welt ist—(wie die Medusa im Palast Rondanini)—, daß so etwas zu machen möglich war, macht einen zum doppelten Menschen!

Die höchste Aufgabe einer jeden Kunst ist, durch den Schein die Täuschung einer höheren Wirklichkeit zu geben. Ein falsches Bestreben aber ist, den Schein so lange zu verwirklichen, bis endlich nur ein gemeines Wirkliche übrigbleibt.

Among the fortunate circumstances that permitted Shakespeare's great innate talent to develop freely and perfectly is the fact that he was a Protestant; otherwise, like Kalidasa and Calderon, he would have had to glorify absurdities.

Just to have an inkling that such works of art exist—like the Medusa in the Palazzo Rondanini—that it is possible to create such things, makes one doubly a man!

It is the highest task of all art to employ appearance to create the illusion of a higher reality. But it is a false endeavor to carry the realization of appearance to such a point as to leave nothing in the end but ordinary reality.

Goethe in Italy
Painting by Wilhelm Tischbein

Wer fremde Sprachen nicht kennt, weiß nichts von seiner eigenen.

He who knows no foreign tongue knows nothing of his own.

Nicht die Sprache an und für sich ist richtig, tüchtig, zierlich, sondern der Geist ist es, der sich darin verkörpert, und so kommt es nicht auf einen jeden an, ob er seinen Rechnungen, Reden oder Gedichten die wünschenswerten Eigenschaften verleihen will: es ist die Frage, ob ihm die Natur hiezu die geistigen und sittlichen Eigenschaften verliehen hat. Die geistigen: das Vermögen der An- und Durchschauung, die sittlichen: daß er die bösen Dämone ablehne, die ihn hindern könnten, dem Wahren die Ehre zu geben.

Ich verfluche allen negativen Purismus, daß man ein Wort nicht brauchen soll, in welchem eine andere Sprache Vieles oder Zarteres gefaßt hat.

Die Muttersprache zugleich reinigen und bereichern ist das Geschäft der besten Köpfe; Reinigung ohne Bereicherung erweist sich öfters geistlos: denn es ist nichts bequemer, als von dem Inhalt absehen und auf den Ausdruck passen. Der geistreiche Mensch knetet seinen Wortstoff, ohne sich zu bekümmern, aus was für Elementen er bestehe, der geistlose hat gut *rein* sprechen, da er nichts zu sagen hat. Wie sollte er fühlen, welches kümmerliche Surrogat er an der Stelle eines bedeutenden Wortes gelten läßt, da ihm jenes Wort nie lebendig war, weil er nichts dabei dachte. Es gibt gar viele Arten von Reinigung und Bereicherung, die eigentlich alle zusammengreifen müssen, wenn die Sprache lebendig wachsen soll. Poesie und leidenschaftliche Rede sind die einzigen Quellen, aus denen dieses Leben hervordringt; und

It is not language itself that is proper, serviceable and graceful, but the spirit embodied in it. Hence it is not up to a person whether he seeks to invest his calculations, speech or verse with the qualities to be desired. The question is whether nature has endowed him with the necessary spiritual and moral qualities. The spiritual qualities are the capacities for perception and insight. The moral quality lies in the rejection of evil demons that might prevent him from doing honor to truth.

A curse upon all negative purism which holds that a broader or subtler term from another language may not be used.

To cleanse and at once enrich the mother tongue is the concern of the best minds. Purification without enrichment often proves barren; for nothing is easier than to concentrate on the proper use of language and lose sight of the content. The fertile mind kneads his verbal clay without troubling about the nature of its constituents, while the barren mind has an easy time of keeping the language pure since he has nothing to say. How could he feel how meager is the substitute he puts in place of a meaningful word? That word was never alive to him, for he never put thought into it. There are indeed many ways of purifying and enriching the language, and they must all interlock if the language is to live and grow. Poetry and passionate speech are the only sources from which such life wells forth; and if, in

sollten sie in ihrer Heftigkeit auch etwas Bergschutt mitführen—er setzt sich zu Boden, und die reine Welle fließt darüber hin.

Die Gewalt einer Sprache ist nicht, daß sie das Fremde abweist, sondern daß sie es verschlingt.

Beim Übersetzen muß man bis ans Unübersetzbare herangehen; alsdann wird man aber erst die fremde Nation und die fremde Sprache gewahr.

Beim Übersetzen muß man sich nur ja nicht in unmittelbaren Kampf mit der fremden Sprache einlassen. Man muß bis an das Unübersetzbare herangehen und dieses respektieren; denn darin liegt eben der Wert und der Charakter einer jeden Sprache.

Der Deutsche soll alle Sprachen lernen, damit ihm zu Hause kein Fremder unbequem, er aber in der Fremde überall zu Hause sei.

Wer die deutsche Sprache versteht und studiert, befindet sich auf dem Markte, wo alle Nationen ihre Waren anbieten, er spielt den Dolmetscher, indem er sich selbst bereichert. Und so ist jeder Übersetzer anzusehen, daß er sich als Vermittler dieses allgemein geistigen Handels bemüht und den Wechseltausch zu fördern sich zum Geschäft macht. Denn was man auch von der Unzulänglichkeit des Übersetzens sagen mag, so ist und bleibt es doch eins der wichtigsten und würdigsten Geschäfte in dem allgemeinen Weltwesen. . . . So ist jeder Übersetzer ein Prophet seinem Volke.

their vehemence, they do carry some sediment, this will settle and the pure flow pass over it.

The power of a language lies not in its rejecting but rather in its devouring what is foreign.

In translation one must proceed to the very limits of the untranslatable; only then does one become aware of the foreign nation and the foreign tongue.

In translating one must not allow oneself to get involved in direct battle with the foreign tongue. One must proceed to the very limits of the untranslatable yet respect them, for in just this lie the value and the character of every language.

Germans should learn all languages. In that way no stranger will irk them at home, while they will be at home everywhere abroad.

Knowing and studying the German language means to enter the marketplace where all nations offer their goods; and whoever plays the role of interpreter grows himself enriched. Every translator must be looked on as an honest broker in this general intellectual trade, concerned with fostering interchange; for whatever one may say about the shortcomings of translation, it remains one of the most important and significant endeavors in the world's work. . . . Indeed, every translator is a prophet to his people.

Mit dem Nationalhaß ist es ein eigenes Ding. Auf den untersten Stufen der Kultur wird man ihn immer am stärksten und heftigsten finden. Es gibt aber eine Stufe, wo er ganz verschwindet und wo man gewissermaßen über den Nationen steht und man ein Glück oder ein Wehe seines Nachbarvolks empfindet, als wäre es dem eigenen begegnet.

It is a curious thing with national hatred. You will always find it most marked and vehement at the lowest stages of culture. Yet there is a stage at which it vanishes altogether, where one stands above the nations, so to speak, sharing joy or sorrow of a neighboring people as though they had been encountered by one's own.

Unsere modernen Kriege machen viele unglücklich, indessen sie dauern, und niemand glücklich, wenn sie vorüber sind.

Der Krieg ist in Wahrheit eine Krankheit, wo die Säfte, die zur Gesundheit und Erhaltung dienen, nur verwendet werden, um ein Fremdes, der Natur Ungemäßes, zu nähren.

Der Patriotismus verdirbt die Geschichte.

Es gibt keine patriotische Kunst und keine patriotische Wissenschaft. Beide gehören, wie alles Hohe, Gute, der ganzen Welt an und können nur durch allgemeine, freie Wechselwirkung aller zugleich Lebenden, in steter Rücksicht auf das, was uns vom Vergangenen übrig und bekannt ist, gefördert werden.

Sowie ein Dichter politisch wirken will, muß er sich einer Partei hingeben, und sowie er dieses tut, ist er als Poet verloren; er muß seinem freien Geiste, seinem unbefangenen Überblick Lebewohl sagen und dagegen die Kappe der Borniertheit und des blinden Hasses über die Ohren ziehen. Der Dichter wird als Mensch und Bürger sein Vaterland lieben, aber das Vaterland seiner poetischen Kräfte und seines poetischen Wirkens ist das Gute, Edle und Schöne, das an keine besondere Provinz und an kein besonderes Land gebunden ist und das er ergreift und bildet, wo er es findet. Er ist darin dem Adler gleich, der mit freiem Blick über Ländern schwebt und dem es

Our modern wars make many unhappy while they last and none happy when they are over.

War is in truth a disease in which the juices that ordinarily serve for the preservation of health are diverted to nourish an excrescence that is foreign to nature.

Patriotism corrupts history.

There is no patriotic art, and no patriotic science. Like all that is sublime and good, both belong to the whole world. They can be fostered only by the free and unlimited interaction of all contemporaries, always paying due respect to the heritage of the past.

No sooner does a poet seek to become politically active than he must surrender to some party, and the moment he does so, he is lost as a poet; he must bid farewell to his free spiirt, to his detached approach, and don instead the fool's cap of blind hatred. As a man and a citizen, the poet will love his country, but the fatherland of his poetic powers and creative work consists of all that is noble and good and beautiful, and that is tied to no particular region, no specific land. He seizes and shapes it wherever he finds it. In this respect he may be likened to the eagle, soaring on high with sweeping gaze, to whom it matters not whether the hare upon

gleichviel wert ist, ob der Hase, auf den er herab-
schießt, in Preußen oder in Sachsen läuft. Und was
heißt denn: sein Vaterland lieben, und was heißt,
patriotisch wirken? Wenn ein Dichter lebenslänglich
bemüht war, schädliche Vorurteile zu bekämpfen,
engherzige Ansichten zu beseitigen, den Geist seines
Volkes aufzuklären, dessen Geschmack zu reinigen
und dessen Gesinnungs- und Denkweise zu veredeln:
was soll er denn da besseres tun? und wie soll er
denn da patriotischer wirken?

Eine wahrhaft allgemeine Duldung wird am sichersten erreicht, wenn man das Besondere der einzelnen
Menschen und Völkerschaften auf sich beruhen läßt,
bei der Überzeugung jedoch festhält, daß das wahrhaft Verdienstliche sich dadurch auszeichnet, daß
es der ganzen Menschheit gehört.

Toleranz sollte eigentlich nur eine vorübergehende
Gesinnung sein: sie muß zur Anerkennung führen.
Dulden heißt beleidigen.

Ich habe weder Blick noch Schritt in fremde Lande
getan als in der Absicht, das allgemein Menschliche,
was über den ganzen Erdboden verbreitet und ver
teilt ist, unter den verschiedensten Formen kennen
zu lernen und solches in meinem Vaterland wieder
zu finden, anzuerkennen und zu fördern.

which it pounces leaps in Prussia or Saxony. And what does it all mean—to love one's country, to be a patriot in deed? A poet who has striven all his life to fight against harmful prejudice, to root out bigotry, to enlighten the spirit of his people, to cleanse their taste and to ennoble their thoughts and convictions—what can he do that would be worthier and how could he show greater love of his country?

A state of true and universal tolerance is best ensured by leaving alone the peculiarities of men and peoples, while maintaining that the truly worthy is distinguished by belonging to all mankind.

Tolerance should, indeed, be but a passing sentiment leading to ultimate acceptance. Continued tolerance is an insult.

I have never cast eyes nor set foot on foreign soil but with the purpose of coming to know, in all its varied forms, the common human element that is spread and shared throughout the world, and of finding it again, acknowledging and fostering it, in my own country.

Offenbar ist das Bestreben der besten Dichter und
ästhetischen Schriftsteller aller Nationen schon seit
geraumer Zeit auf das allgemein Menschliche gerichtet. In jedem Besondern . . . wird man durch Na-
tionalität und Persönlichkeit hindurch jenes Allgemeine immer mehr durchleuchten und durchschim-
mern sehen.

Ich halte es für wahr, daß die Humanität endlich
siegen wird, nur fürcht' ich, daß zu gleicher Zeit
die Welt ein großes Hospital und einer des andern
humaner Krankenwärter werden wird.

Manifestly the finest poets and creative writers of all nations have for some time now directed their endeavors to the concerns of mankind as a whole. Through all the differences conditioned by nationality and personality, this trend toward the general shines through more and more.

I think it is true that humanity will win out in the end, but I am afraid that at the same time the world will become one great hospital, with each his fellow's kindly nurse.

Zum Sehen geboren,
Zum Schauen bestellt,
Dem Turme geschworen,
Gefällt mir die Welt.
Ich blick' in die Ferne,
Ich seh' in der Näh'
Den Mond und die Sterne,
Den Wald und das Reh.
So seh' ich in allen
Die ewige Zier,
Und wie mir's gefallen,
Gefall' ich auch mir.
Ihr glücklichen Augen,
Was je ihr gesehn,
Es sei, wie es wolle,
Es war doch so schön!

Conceived to be seeing,
Appointed to sight,
The tower my being,
The world my delight.
I peer in the distance,
I see what is near,
The heavens' persistence,
The fleet-footed deer.
And as I find measure
In all that I view,
I view it with pleasure
And so myself too.
Ye eyes I call blessed,
Of all things ye see
The lasting remembrance
Their beauty will be.

Neue Erfindungen können und werden geschehen, allein es kann nichts Neues ausgedacht werden, was auf den sittlichen Menschen Bezug hat.

Das überhandnehmende Maschinenwesen quält und ängstigt mich; es wälzt sich heran wie ein Gewitter, langsam, langsam, aber es hat seine Richtung genommen, es wird kommen und treffen.

Reichtum und Schnelligkeit ist, was die Welt bewundert und wonach jeder strebt; Eisenbahnen, Schnellposten, Dampfschiffe und alle möglichen Fazilitäten der Kommunikation sind es, worauf die gebildete Welt ausgeht, sich zu überbieten, zu überbilden und dadurch in der Mittelmäßigkeit zu verharren. Und das ist ja auch das Resultat der Allgemeinheit, daß eine mittlere Kultur gemein werde. . . . Eigentlich ist das Jahrhundert für die fähigen Köpfe, für leichtfassende und praktische Menschen, die, mit einer gewissen Gewandtheit ausgestattet, ihre Superiorität über die Menge fühlen, wenn sie gleich selbst nicht zum Höchsten begabt sind. . . . Laßt uns soviel als möglich an der Gesinnung halten, in der wir herankamen; wir werden, mit vielleicht noch wenigen, die Letzten sein einer Epoche, die sobald nicht wiederkehrt.

Humboldt hat mit großer Sachkenntnis noch andere Punkte angegeben, wo man mit Benutzung einiger in den Mexikanischen Meerbusen strömender Flüsse vielleicht noch vorteilhafter zum Ziel käme als bei Panama. Dies ist nun alles der Zukunft und einem

New inventions are possible and will be made, but it is not possible to think up anything new with respect to man as a moral being.

I am tormented and terrified by the sweeping growth of machinery. It rolls on like a storm, slowly, slowly, but it has taken its bearing, it will arrive, and it will strike.

Wealth and speed are what the world admires, what each pursues. Railways, express mails, steamships and every possible facility for communication are the achievement in which the civilized world vies and revels, only to languish in mediocrity by that very fact. Indeed, the effect of this diffusion is to spread a culture of the mediocre. . . . This is truly the century for able heads, for practical people with a ready grasp, who, equipped with a certain facility, sense their superiority over the masses, even though they lack the highest endowment. . . . Let us as much as possible cling to the convictions in which we were nurtured. We, with perhaps a very few others, are likely to be the last representatives of an epoch that will not soon return.

Humboldt, possessed of a profound knowledge of the subject, has mentioned still other points where one might take advantage of several rivers flowing into the Gulf of Mexico and attain the goal even better than at Panama. All this must now be left

großen Unternehmungsgeist vorbehalten. Soviel aber ist gewiß, gelänge ein Durchstich der Art, daß man mit Schiffen von jeder Ladung und jeder Größe durch solchen Kanal aus dem Mexikanischen Meerbusen in den Stillen Ozean fahren könnte, so würden daraus für die ganze zivilisierte und nichtzivilisierte Menschheit ganz unberechenbare Resultate hervorgehen. Wundern sollte es mich aber, wenn die Vereinigten Staaten es sich sollten entgehen lassen, ein solches Werk in die Hände zu bekommen. Es ist vorauszusehen, daß dieser jugendliche Staat, bei seiner entschiedenen Tendenz nach Westen, in dreißig bis vierzig Jahren auch die großen Landstrecken jenseits der Felsengebirge in Besitz genommen und bevölkert haben wird. Es ist ferner vorauszusehen, daß an dieser ganzen Küste des Stillen Ozeans, wo die Natur bereits die geräumigsten und sichersten Häfen gebildet hat, nach und nach sehr bedeutende Handelsstädte entstehen werden, zur Vermittlung eines großen Verkehrs zwischen China nebst Ostindien und den Vereinigten Staaten. In solchem Fall wäre es aber nicht bloß wünschenswert, sondern fast notwendig, daß sowohl Handels- wie Kriegsschiffe zwischen der nordamerikanischen westlichen und östlichen Küste eine raschere Verbindung unterhielten, als es bisher durch die langweilige, widerwärtige und kostspielige Fahrt um das Kap Horn möglich gewesen. Ich wiederhole also: es ist für die Vereinigten Staaten durchaus unerläßlich, daß sie eine Durchfahrt aus dem Mexikanischen Meerbusen in den Stillen Ozean bewerkstelligen, und ich bin gewiß, daß sie es erreichen.

to the future and its burgeoning spirit of enterprise. This much, however, is certain: If a cut were successfully made, such that ships of every size and cargo could sail through this canal from the Gulf of Mexico to the Pacific Ocean, altogether incalculable results would flow from it, for all mankind, civilized and uncivilized alike. I should be indeed surprised if the United States were to miss the chance of getting such an undertaking into its hands. It is foreseeable that this youthful country, with its marked westward trend, will have taken possession and populated the great land areas beyond the Rocky Mountains within thirty to forty years as well. It is further foreseeable that very important commercial centers will arise along this entire Pacific coast, where nature has already shaped spacious and secure harbors—which cities will serve a great trade between the United States and China, in addition to East India. In such an eventuality it would be not merely desirable but almost indispensable that merchant as well as naval vessels maintain a faster route between the west and east coasts of North America than has been possible heretofore by the overlong, hazardous and costly journey around Cape Horn. Hence I repeat: it is absolutely essential for the United States to effect a shortcut from the Gulf of Mexico into the Pacific Ocean, and I am certain it will succeed in doing so.

Dieses möchte ich erleben; aber ich werde es nicht. Zweitens möchte ich erleben, eine Verbindung der Donau mit dem Rhein hergestellt zu sehen. Aber dieses Unternehmen ist gleichfalls so riesenhaft, daß ich an der Ausführung zweifle, zumal in Erwägung unserer deutschen Mittel. Und endlich drittens möchte ich die Engländer im Besitz eines Kanals von Suez sehen. Diese drei großen Dinge möchte ich erleben, und es wäre wohl der Mühe wert, ihnen zuliebe noch einige funfzig Jahre auszuhalten.

Wirken wir fort, bis wir . . . vom Weltgeist berufen, in den Äther zurückkehren! Möge dann der ewig Lebendige uns neue Tätigkeiten, denen analog, in welchen wir uns schon erprobt, nicht versagen! . . .

I should like to live to see this, but I shall not. I should like, secondly, to live to see a connection created between the Danube and the Rhine. Yet this undertaking too is so gigantic that I doubt its execution, especially considering our German means. And thirdly, I should like to see the English in possession of a canal at Suez. These three great things I should like to live to see, and for their sake it might well be worth the effort to hold out another fifty years or so.

Let us carry on our work until we . . . summoned by the world spirit, return to the ether! Then may the Ever Living not deny us new activities, like unto those in which we have tested ourselves. . . .

Die Zukunft decket
Schmerzen und Glücke
schrittweis dem Blicke,
doch ungeschrecket
dringen wir vorwärts.

Und schwer und ferne
hängt eine Hülle
mit Ehrfurcht.—Stille
ruhn oben die Sterne
und unten die Gräber.

Doch rufen von drüben
die Stimmen der Geister,
die Stimmen der Meister:
"Versäumt nicht zu üben
die Kräfte des Guten!

Hier flechten sich Kronen
in ewiger Stille,
die sollen mit Fülle
die Tätigen lohnen!
Wir heißen euch hoffen!"

The future holds hidden
Blessings and sorrows
In rows of tomorrows.—
Undaunted, unbidden
We keep pressing forward.

Heavy and far
Of awe a curtain.
Star beyond star
Above. And certain
The graves below.

But voices we hallow
Of masters preceding
Invoke our heeding:
"Let never lie fallow
The forces of good.

We gather forever
In infinite calm
The laurel, the palm
For lives of endeavor—
And bid you have hope."

Ja! diesem Sinne bin ich ganz ergeben,
Das ist der Weisheit letzter Schluß:
Nur der verdient sich Freiheit wie das Leben,
Der täglich sie erobern muß.

This I believe with passionate obsession
And call it wisdom's ultimate advice:
None keeps of life and liberty possession,
But daily pays in sweat and toil their price.

Goethe's garden house in Weimar

Life mask of Goethe, 1807

CHRONICLE OF
GOETHE'S LIFE AND WORKS

Born on August 28, 1749 at Frankfurt am Main, son of Johann Kaspar Goethe and his wife Katharine Elisabeth, daughter of Johann Wolfgang Textor, Mayor of Frankfurt.

1765-68

University of Leipzig. Return home with health ruined by youthful excesses and "with the feelings of one shipwrecked."

Buch Annette [handwritten volume of poems to Anna Katharina Schönkopf]. *Die Laune des Verliebten* [The Whim of the Infatuated, pastoral play].

1768-70

Frankfurt am Main. Pietistic meetings. Influence of Susanne von Klettenberg, family friend. First interest in the natural sciences.

Die Mitschuldigen [The Accomplices, a comedy].

1770-71

University of Strassburg. Acquaintance with Herder. Friederike Brion, daughter of the parson of Sesenheim.

Poems to Friederike. Collection of folk songs.

1771-72

Frankfurt am Main. Acquaintance with J. H. Merck and his friends in Darmstadt.

Faust (Urfaust) [first version] begun. History of Gottfried of Berlichingen dramatized.

1772

Wetzlar (district court) Charlotte Buff. J. C. Kestner.

1772-75

Frankfurt am Main. Acquaintance with Lavater, F. H. Jacobi. Klopstock, the Counts Stolberg.

Götz von Berlichingen published anonymously, 1773.

1774

Engagement to Lili Schöne-mann (later dissolved).

Clavigo (a tragedy). *The Sufferings of Young Werther (Die Leiden des jungen Werthers)*, a novel.

1775

May-July: First trip to Switzerland, November 7: arrival in Weimar. Duke Carl August von Sachsen-Weimar. K. L. von Knebel, Wieland, Herder. Goethe takes over most branches of the duchy's administration.

Erwin und Elmire (a musical play). *Stella* (A Play for Lovers), 1876.

1776-88

Friendship with Charlotte von Stein.

Wilhelm Meisters theatralische Sendung (Urmeister) [Wilhelm Meister's theatrical mission] 1777-85.

1779-1780

September 1779 - January 1780: second trip to Switzerland.

Iphigenie in Tauris (first version) 1779.

1782

Raised to nobility by the Emperor.

1786-88

First Italian trip.

1786

October 29: arrival in Rome. Boarding with the painter J. H. W. Tischbein. Angelika Kauffmann. J. H. Meyer, painter and writer, friend of his later years. K. P. Moritz (Berlin art philosopher).

1787

February: Naples, Vesuvius, Pompeii. March: Palermo, Girgenti, Catania, Taormina, Messina. May: Naples. June: Rome.

Iphigenie in Tauris.

1788

April 25: departure from Rome. Florence, Milan, Lake Como.

Egmont (a tragedy).

1788-92

Weimar.
Christiane Vulpius.

1790

March-June: Trip to Venice.

On the Metamorphosis of Plants.

1791-1817

Director of the Weimar Theatre.

Torquato Tasso, 1790.
Faust, a fragment, 1790.
Contributions to Optics, 1791-92.

1792

Campaign in France. Cannonade of Valmy.

Der Grosskophta [The Grand Cophta, a comedy].

1793

Siege of Mainz.

Der Bürgergeneral [The Citizen-General, a comedy]. *Reinecke Fuchs* [Reynard the Fox, epic poem], 1794.

1794-1805

Friendship with Schiller.

Römische Elegien [Roman elegies, in Schiller's Horen], 1795. *Unterhaltungen deutscher Ausgewanderten* [Discussions of German Emigrees], 1795. *Wilhelm Meister's Apprenticeship* (Wilhelm Meisters Lehrjahre), 1795-96. *Xenia* (with Schiller), 1797. *Hermann und Dorothea*, 1798.

1797

Third trip to Switzerland.

Die Propyläen (periodical), 1798-1800. *Die natürliche Tochter* [The Natural Daughter, a tragedy], 1804. *Pandora* (a festival play). *Des Epimenides Erwachen* [Epimenides' Awakening, a festival play].

1805

Schiller dies.

1806

Marries Christiane.

Faust, First Part, 1808. *Elective Affinities* (Die Wahlverwandtschaften). 1809.

Zur Farbenlehre (Theory of Colors), 1809. *Dichtung und Wahrheit* [Poetry and Truth, ˙ autobiography], 1811-32.

1816

Christiane dies.

Über Kunst und Altertum [On Art and Antiquity, periodical], 1816-32. *Italienische Reise* (Italian Journey), 1816-17. *Morphologie* (Morphology), 1817-23. *West-östlicher Divan* (West-Eastern Divan), 1819. *Wilhelm Meister's Journeying Years* (Wilhelm Meisters Wanderjahre), 1822.

1823

J. P. Eckerman becomes Goethe's secretary and collaborator.

Novelle [Novella], 1828. *Correspondence of Schiller and Goethe.* 1828-29. *Wilhelm Meister's Journeying Years.* (Wilhelm Meisters Wanderjahre) (Second version), 1829. *Annalen, Tages- und Jahres-Hefte* [Annals— Day and Year Books], 1830. *Faust,* Second Part, 1832.

Goethe's death: March 22, 1832

Goethe's home in Weimar

The following selections were taken from *Anthology of German Poetry through the 19th Century*, also published by Frederick Ungar:

Translated by Alexander Gode

page 29, sixth item	page 107
31, first, second, third	115
	129, second, third item
65, fifth	
67, third	131, sixth
69, fifth	141, fourth
75, fifth	145, sixth
89, fourth	193
95	199, third, to 201
	203

Translated by Albert Bloch
page 31, seventh item

Illustrations for frontispiece, pages 177 and 206 are from Bruckmann-Art Reference Bureau. Those on pages 49, 93, 205, and 213 are from Marburg-Art Reference Bureau.